REMOVING REBELLION'S ROOTS

"In this intensely practical, theologically rich book, Olan Stubbs gets down to the 'why' of our wandering from God. This is not a mere slap on the hand for reaching into sin's cookie jar but an invitation to enjoy the feast of God's abundant goodness. As a pastor I look forward to sharing this with both new believers and struggling, seasoned saints."

—**Chris Davis**, Senior Pastor, Groveton Baptist Church

"Olan Stubbs has drawn on years of experience discipling college students, mature Christians, and ministry leaders to write a wise and helpful book that helps us grow in holiness and grace by attacking the roots of sin. Stubbs takes readers on a journey through Scripture, through centuries of Christian wisdom, and through reflection on contemporary experience, to discern the sources of sin, beginning with Satan's lies. Join him in the paths of progress—and treasure the appendices, which are worth the price of the book."

—**Dan Doriani**, Professor of Biblical Theology, Covenant Seminary

"Satan's number one weapon to steal, kill, and destroy is deception, and our natural tendency to self-deceive makes us incredibly vulnerable to his lies. If we are going to live a life of freedom and victory like Jesus promised, we must be dialed into this reality. This book will not only help you identify the lies that are foundational to your sin struggles. It will also instruct you how to use the truth of God's word to progressively bring freedom in your life from the sins that so easily entangle you."

—**Ted Shimer**, Founder, The Freedom Fight

"If the doctrines of grace have become just an abstraction to you with little sense of spiritual warfare, Dr. Olan Stubbs will help you in making these 'truth wars' a living reality to your heart. Beyond offering simple solutions to attaining spiritual freedom, this book invariably removes obstacles and cultivates that 'hunger and thirst after righteousness' which is the only indispensable condition to being 'filled.' Dr. Stubbs is eminently and always scriptural and expository. He starts with the word and expounds it. It is exposition at its very best and highest."

—**Robert Davis Smart**, Spiritual Formation Pastor At Large, Christ Church (PCA), Bloomington, Illinois

"Olan has provided the Christian community with another helpful tool. With great clarity, he teaches pew dwellers how to understand the war within, recognize the tactics of the devil, and use biblical tools to correct their thinking, which gives rise to their vulnerability to the enemy. As a biblical counselor with more than fifty years of counseling experience, as I read, I thought many times that Olan had been eavesdropping in my office—he echoed the biblical counsel offered. He does this in a contemporary, readable style."

—**Howard Eyrich**, Director, Doctor of Ministry Program, Birmingham Theological Seminary

REMOVING REBELLION'S ROOTS

Seeing and Severing Satan's Lies
with the Sword of God's Word

OLAN STUBBS

Foreword by Harrison Perkins

WIPF & STOCK · Eugene, Oregon

REMOVING REBELLION'S ROOTS
Seeing and Severing Satan's Lies with the Sword of God's Word

Copyright © 2025 Olan Stubbs. All rights reserved. Except for brief quotations in critical publications or reviews, no part of this book may be reproduced in any manner without prior written permission from the publisher. Write: Permissions, Wipf and Stock Publishers, 199 W. 8th Ave., Suite 3, Eugene, OR 97401.

Wipf & Stock
An Imprint of Wipf and Stock Publishers
199 W. 8th Ave., Suite 3
Eugene, OR 97401

www.wipfandstock.com

PAPERBACK ISBN: 979-8-3852-4338-9
HARDCOVER ISBN: 979-8-3852-4339-6
EBOOK ISBN: 979-8-3852-4340-2

VERSION NUMBER 09/08/25

Unless otherwise stated, Scripture quotation are taken from The Holy Bible, New American Standard Bible, copyright 1977 by The Lockman Foundation. Used by permission. All rights reserved.

All hymns used are public domain.

This book is dedicated to my four kids, whom I pray will know how to fight Satan's lies with the truth of God's good word. I love you all so much.

Contents

Foreword by Harrison Perkins | ix
Acknowledgments | xi
Introduction | xiii

1. How to Be Holy | 1
2. Sin Starts with Satan | 14
3. Lies Rooted in Reality | 31
4. Layers of Lies | 48
5. Killing Coveting | 63
6. Sin After the Sin | 80
7. Accused and Acquitted | 96
8. Conspiracy of Circumstances | 110
9. Forgiven to Be Free | 125
10. Fight for Faith | 144
11. Faith vs. Fear | 157

Conclusion | 167

Appendix A: Sinful Self-Protective Strategies | 169
Appendix B: Confronting Someone in Order to Forgive Them and Set Boundaries | 172
Appendix C: Satan's Five Main Lies and Accusations and Our Responses | 174
Appendix D: Overview and Summary | 176
Appendix E: Questions to Ask Yourself and Others to Help Discern Personalized Lies | 178

Bibliography | 179

Foreword

In his high priestly prayer, Christ prayed to the Father for his people, "They are not of the world, just as I am not of the world. Sanctify them in the truth; your word is truth" (John 17:16–17 ESV). Throughout John's Gospel and in his epistles, this language of being not of the world refers to the ethical difference that God's people are supposed to have from those who have not (at least not yet) been given new life (e.g., 1 John 2:15–17). Following his statement that his people by grace are not of the world, and so are ethically distinct, Jesus petitioned that the Father would sanctify his people *in the truth*. Christ understood that an inextricable connection bound the truth together with how Christ's people are divinely set apart.

Olan Stubbs also understands that the truth has an intrinsic role to play in how we are able to move forward in holiness in the Christian life. Throughout this book, he continually unwraps biblical insights and practical strategies for how Christ's prayer that we would be sanctified *in the truth* come to bear upon our walk with the Lord. Stubbs points us to the reality that, since God is truth, the truth is good for us as well as satisfying. The lie that undergirds all temptation is that we would be happier in sin than in following God's moral law. Yet, this book shows us how that lie actually leads us toward misery and away from the truth that God would have good things for his people, but those good things are not found in the paths of sin.

We might all find it too easy to believe that holiness is a life of stinginess. Even too many Christians buy into the lie that God is out to squish our fun by instructing us to follow him in godliness. In this respect, the devil is that liar who would have us believe that sin is rewarding and that ungodliness is satisfying. He would further have us believe a host of other lies about God, about ourselves, and about our relationship with God that make it easier for him to deceive us with those lies about whether holiness or sinfulness is truly where satisfaction in how we live might be found.

What a privilege it is, then, for me to commend Olan Stubbs's book to you as a guide for recognizing how lies come at us and for diagnosing the lies we are personally prone to believe. Olan has for years been a trusted guide and confidant for me both in matters of fighting against sin and especially in overcoming lies I easily believe about myself—lies that are contrary to God's goodness and to the gospel itself. I am glad that his teaching, which has so often blessed my soul, is available for wider audiences.

Harrison Perkins
Oakland Hills Community Church

Acknowledgments

I would once again like to thank Wipf and Stock for working with me to publish this book. I would like to thank Harrison Perkins for writing the foreword, helping me with editing, and encouraging me to write. I would also like to thank Bob Smart who taught me some of the foundational principles in this book.

I also want to thank my wife and four kids for supporting me, encouraging me, actually reading some of my books, and giving me time to write. I love you all so much and am so grateful for you. Mostly, I thank the Lord Jesus Christ. Anything good or right or true in me or around me or that comes through me is all ultimately from and unto him. To Christ be the glory.

Introduction

Whack-A-Mole Sanctification

Whack-A-Mole is an arcade game where you continually have to "whack" mechanical moles to win the game. I remember it was popular at Chuck E. Cheese pizza restaurant when I used to take my young kids. The player stands in front of a table of sorts with many different holes. You hold a soft mallet in your hands. As the game begins, motorized "moles" pop out of the different holes at various times and the goal is to hit them on the head before they go back into the hole on their own. You gain points by whacking a mole. The problem is, no matter how good you are at the game, no matter how fast you whack those moles, another mole will always pop up somewhere again until the game is over. Often a mole you just whacked might seem to pop up soon again from the very same hole.

Unfortunately, this game resembles the Christian life for all believers. We know God desires us to live practically righteous lives. We desire to be righteous (at least some of the time). We want to do our part. We know we have a part to play. So, as we see the evil fruits of sin pop up in our life, we are quick to cut them off. We install porn blockers on our phones to protect our eyes and that is a great idea. (I have one.) If we tend to drink too much, we make sure not to keep alcohol at our house. Maybe if we are given to using foul language, we put money in a jar any time we cuss.

We also pray, fast, confess our sins, and go to church. We use the normal means of grace. We listen to the word of God preached and seek to apply it. We are serious about our use of the Lord's Supper. But we often feel that our progress is slow and painful at best. Why is that?

INTRODUCTION

For many of us, we spend too much time and effort focused on the sinful fruit and not enough time focused on the root of sin itself. I have written this book to try to help Christians bring real power to attack the deepest roots of their sin. God's grace and power, rightly applied, is like lethal poison to the sin that still dwells in our hearts.

We need to dig deep around the tree of our lives. To see progress, we must go as far down to the depths of where our sin starts in our thoughts, affections, desires, and will. And there, with the help of the Holy Spirit, we must apply gospel truth in such a way as to sever the roots of our sin so that the fruit will show up less and less.

No one is ever going to be 100 percent sinlessly perfect in this life until Christ returns (Eccl 7:20). None of us can ever say that we have truly and fully loved God with all our heart, soul, mind, and strength perfectly (Mark 12:30). But we can make real, significant, noticeable sustained progress in practical obedience to God. The goal of this book is to help you go as far as you can in this life in being conformed to the image of Christ (Rom 8:29).

I would encourage you to read this book with others so that you can discuss what you are learning and have accountability for what you seek to apply. I have recorded and uploaded sermons to PodBean that follow the chapters of this book.[1] There is also a workbook, entitled *Truth Wars*, that goes along with the sermons with questions that may be helpful as well.[2]

The first chapter will show us how much our personal holiness is rooted in the truths we believe about God, ourselves, and life in general. Chapter 2 will show us how Satan seeks to attack God's truth. He came to Adam and Eve in the garden with lies about God, humanity, and all of life. He is still seeking to lie to people today. All of life is a war between God's truth and Satan's lies. This war is fought largely in our minds.

Chapter 3 shows us that Satan's lies are not random nor arbitrary. He is a master of rooting our lies in the reality we experience. Satan has delegated authority from God to use circumstances to try and convince us his lies are true.

Chapter 4 shows us how Satan will use multiple lies to try and draw us away from our relationship with God. He doesn't care if he lures us into outwardly scandalous sin or into mere inward smug self-righteousness,

---

1. See https://gospeltalk.podbean.com/category/killing-sin-s-roots. Chapter 1 corresponds to the sermon uploaded on Tuesday, June 6, 2022.

2. See Stubbs, *Truth Wars* on amazon.com.

if he can lure us away from simple faith in the Lord. Chapter 5 shows us how coveting plays an important role in sin. Once Satan has convinced us that God won't provide for us sufficiently, he begins to convince us we must provide for ourselves. Once we have bought into that lie, we begin to lust after things in life we believe will bring us security, satisfaction, and significance.

Once we have sinned outwardly Satan doesn't leave us alone. Then he seeks to condemn us. Chapter 6 shows how our first response is not to run to Christ and beg mercy as we should. Rather we are tempted to sinfully self-protect ourselves with further lies and self-righteousness.

Chapter 7 illustrates how Satan continues to accuse those who have genuine saving faith in God. Satan does not give up easily. He pursues us relentlessly in the war of our minds.

The eighth chapter shows how Satan pursued Christ throughout his life. He never gave up. He sought for Christ's weak points and sought to exploit them. Satan does the same in his pursuit of us.

Chapter 9 shows how forgiving others who have sinned against us can be a huge practical step in experiencing the freedom Christ has purchased for us. Satan's lies are counteracted by the gospel of grace. To fully experience this grace, we must seek to practice it in our relationship with others who have hurt us.

Chapters 10 and 11 give us two biblical examples of people pursued by Satan. We see how they struggle with sin and yet eventually find freedom through the grace of Christ. Several appendixes follow to help you apply these truths to your life. The goal is to experience real lasting freedom from besetting sins. Thomas Brooks wisely states, "Christ, the Scripture, your own hearts, and Satan's devices, are the four prime things that should be our first and most studied and searched. If any cast off the study of these, they cannot be safe here, nor happy hereafter."[3] Hopefully this book will help us all be safe and holy in life, and happy in Christ in the next life.

---

3. Brooks, *Precious Remedies*, 15.

Chapter 1

How to Be Holy

Genesis 2:16–25

This book is about how to attack sin at the deepest level. The goal is to understand at the deepest level the true roots of our sin. Then, by God's grace and with his help, we want to do all we can to eradicate sin in our lives.

This process will never be finished in this life. The sanctification battle will continue until we see Jesus face-to-face in glory. And yet we can and must fight against indwelling sin with all our heart, soul, mind, and strength. If we genuinely love Christ, then we will do all we can to obey his commands (John 14:15).

Often in life and in the Bible, we see people attacking sin at the fruit rather than the root. It is easy to take a symptomatic approach to sin that never really addresses the heart of the issue. Thus, we find ourselves playing a lifelong, exhausting game of whack-a-mole with our sin. And it is not incredibly fun. In fact, it is a guaranteed recipe to lose the battle. Eventually you will exhaust yourself, give up, and the "moles" of sin will win.

Merely cutting off the fruits of our sinfulness does not really change us from the inside out. This book is written to help us make real progress in the fight against sin. We will start by trying to understand the goal of true godliness.

Oftentimes our view of sinfulness is too small, narrow, and short-sighted. This is often the case because our view of our holiness is also far too truncated. In this chapter we want to try to get a clear biblical picture of godliness. Only three people have ever lived any amount of time on this planet in a sinless fashion. We will look at them in this chapter.

True holiness, at a minimum, consists of trusting, obeying, and enjoying. Let's see how this played out in Eden. Let's seek to learn how this can be applied in our own lives as well.

TRUSTING

When God first made humankind, he put him into a garden to cultivate and care for it but also to enjoy it. God spoke to Adam and told him that he could eat freely from the fruit of any tree of the garden except one special tree. When we read or remember the Genesis account we often, understandably so, focus on this one prohibition. But we must not forget that the God that gave one clear no from the beginning also gave many more yeses! He is a good God, a great Father, who loves to give good gifts to his children.

In the Hebrew, Gen 2:16 says from all trees of the garden you may "eat eat." It is the Hebraic way to emphasis something. God was showing off his lavish generosity. Yes, he was commanding Adam to live and work in the garden and thus serve God. But just as much, if not more, he promised to provide for Adam. He was not promising to provide for him in some bare minimum way but rather in an extravagant way. God owns all things and enjoys sharing with his children!

Genesis 2 refers to God as the LORD God. Most English translations of the Bible use LORD (in all caps) to show the personal name of God, Yahweh. This is a way to remind us that God is a relational God. He is a covenant making and covenant keeping God. The essence of the relationship in Gen 2 was God saying to Adam, "I will be your God, and you will be my servant. You will serve me and obey, and I will bless and satisfy you."

God has been and will continue to be a relational God from eternity past into infinity and beyond. From the beginning God is Trinity. He is God the Father, God the Son, and God the Holy Spirit. He is God three in one, one in three.

God did not create humanity out of any lack, need, weakness, boredom, or loneliness. It would be more accurate to say that God has been having an eternal party of joy and love within himself for all eternity. His decision to create human beings was borne out of a desire to enter fellowship with humans. The love and joy the Trinity has eternally shared is so wonderful God decided to make humanity and invite us to join their party.

God is the perfect Father. God is attentive to and prepared for the needs and desires of Adam. It is as if God says, "Adam, look at all I have prepared for you. Look at all I have provided! There's water and sunshine. There is moonlight and beauty. There are fruits and vegetables. Eat your fill! Eat freely of all the tasty foods I invented for you. Enjoy my creation, made for you!"

But there was one tree that was off limits. God never gives a reason or explanation as to why it was off limits. The bottom line is that it was off limits just because God said so. We may not like it when parents say this. And yet if any parent in the world has a right to say this to his kids it is Yahweh the Creator and owner of all things.

It's highly likely that there was nothing poisonous or wrong with the tree in and of itself. Rather, it serves almost a sacramental purpose. Sacraments are outward signs of inward realities wherein God uses some earthly thing to display spiritual things. In the new covenant, we have baptism and the Lord's Supper as our sacraments. Normal water in baptism signifies a spiritual cleansing. Normal bread and wine signify the body and blood of Christ as well as our communion and fellowship with him. Likewise, the tree in the garden was used sacramentally as a test for humankind. It was to help man determine the difference in good and evil. This tree symbolically encapsulated whether Adam would obey God in all things.

The best and right way to determine the difference in good and evil is to hear, believe, and obey God's word. Trusting God and obeying him is good and right. Not trusting God and disobeying him is evil. That is the ultimate dividing line between all behavior.

John Stott says, "The essence of sin is godlessness. It is an attempt to get rid of God, and since that is impossible, the determination to live as though one had succeeded in doing so."[1] The essence of righteousness is godliness or living in alignment with God. The essence of sin is godlessness or living out of alignment with your Creator.

If God says something is good, it is good. If God says something is evil, it is evil, full stop. That is the end of the story. There is no debate. It does not matter if we like it or not. It does not matter if we agree or understand. It is God's world and thus God's rules.

Sinclair Ferguson is extremely helpful on this point. "They were to show their love for him by refusing to eat the fruit of only one tree, on

---

1. Stott, *Romans*, 72.

the basis that their loving Father said so[,] . . . a command added to the instinctive obedience that was written into their constitution as the image of God."[2]

The deepest root of holiness is simply trusting God. Romans 14:23 says "whatever is not from faith is sin." Tim Keller says, "All sin against God is grounded in a refusal to believe that God is more dedicated to our good, and more aware of what that is, than we are."[3] Martyn Lloyd-Jones agrees: "The ultimate cause of all spiritual depression is unbelief."[4] True faith trusts that God is wiser than we are and more loving than we are. True faith believes that God knows us better than we know ourselves (he did create us after all!) and that he loves us more than we love ourselves.

Look at the times and seasons in your life where you rebelled against God. How did it work out for you? Are you proud of those times? Would you like to return and repeat them the same way again? Most of us, if we are honest, have seasons in our life where we clearly called the shots in our lives and didn't let God lead us. And those times of self-leadership almost always end in absolute disaster. To the extent that they don't or didn't, it is just a clear reminder of the undeserved grace and mercy and goodness of God.

When we do truly humble ourselves and trust in God, what is the result? The first result is that we practically obey him. If we persevere in such obedience, blessings will always come in the long run, but not always in the short run.

OBEYING

It is never enough in life to say, "Of course I believe in and trust God. So, now I can go and do whatever the heck I want!" Most of us would never say that out loud with our mouths, but we often say it with our life decisions.

James famously said, "Faith without works is dead" (Jas 2:26). Read Jas 2:18–20 for further context. This is the clear repeated teaching of the entire Bible and, honestly, of life experience. Frank Barker, who used to be my pastor at Briarwood Presbyterian Church, used to say, "It's not about the perfection of your life. It is about the direction of your life."

2. Ferguson, *Whole Christ*, 68.
3. Keller, *Prodigal Prophet*, 137–39.
4. Lloyd-Jones, *Spiritual Depressions*, 20.

If someone genuinely trusts in God, that will inevitably lead to obeying God. None of us will ever perfectly obey God in this life. But to the degree that we truly trust him, we will also obey. If you go to see a doctor and he prescribes a certain medical treatment, how will you respond? If you fully trust the doctor, you will do what he told you to do. If you doubt the wisdom of the doctor, you will be slow or reluctant to obey.

If Adam and Eve had truly and fully trusted God in the garden of Eden, they would have obeyed. They would have cared for the garden. They would have fellowshipped with God. They would have eaten their fill from every tree in the garden save one. They would have had a happy marriage and lots of children. It seems simple, doesn't it? One commentator says that "man had all he required."[5] They lacked no good thing for a happy, healthy, productive life. They had no legitimate reason to disobey. Why would anyone go looking for something prohibited when you have all you need for life and godliness and more?!

Some people reading this book may understand the importance of obedience in the Christian life. Some may go as far as to say that they understand it too well! By this they may mean that they tend to overemphasis the importance of obedience in the Christian life. That's not a bad thing to emphasize, if it is not the only part of life in Christ you emphasize.

There are many who for assorted reasons want to minimize the importance of obedience. That is certainly not the direction the Bible takes us. There are certainly rules in the Bible. The first rule was not to eat the fruit of the forbidden tree. Sometimes people try to pit rules against a relationship when it comes to spirituality. But it's better to say that God has given his people rules in the context of a loving and gracious relationship. In that context the right rules are glorious! "His commandments are not burdensome" (1 John 5:3b). God created Adam and Eve to be in a relationship with him. From the very beginning of that relationship there were rules to help govern that relationship such as not eating from one certain tree. In a similar fashion parents have children. There is a natural and obvious relationship between parent and child. But as soon as the child begins to mature, that child will understand there are rules operating in the relationship such as the child must obey the parent, etc.

It is not accidental that I have three main points in the first chapter on how to be holy. Nor is it accidental that the middle point is about

---

5. Wenham, *Genesis 1–15*, 72.

obedience. It's not the first point. It's not the last point. I don't think it's the most crucial point. But it is a vital point that does get to the heart of our relationship with the Lord.

A right relationship with God starts with faith. It leads to obedience. But it does not end there. There is much more!

Bare minimum, slavish, begrudging obedience is never enough. In one sense it is not even real obedience. God does not want mere external conformity to his word. Rather, he wants us to love his words with our heart, soul, mind, and strength. He wants us to obey willingly, gladly, joyfully. God is the best parent of all time. All parents ideally want their children to obey them with a glad heart and a motivation of love and with a smile on their face.

We start with faith. This leads to obedience. Rightly done, this should eventually lead to joy!

ENJOYING

Before the prohibition in Gen 2:17, God gave a great release, a great word of freedom! One commentator said, "God begins with a great release."[6] John Calvin states, "For not only was there an abundant supply of food, but with it was added sweetness for the gratification of the palate, and beauty to feast the eyes. . . . To the end that Adam might the more willingly comply, God commends his own liberality."[7] Ferguson reminds us, "God had commanded our first parents to enjoy. The positive statement is as much part of the command as the negative."[8]

God knew Adam would be tempted to sin. Thus, he gave Adam extra motivation beyond a mere "because I told you so!" You might even say God blessed his socks off if Adam hadn't been naked! He filled his life with sweet and good things that Adam would enjoy, hopefully causing him to pause and worship, and remember and realize even more fully what a great God he had!

I went to Epcot in Orlando Florida. It is one of Disney's theme parks. At the time, they had a theater designed to highlight the glories of the state of California. You sit in a huge room with a screen that literally surrounds you. They showed beautiful pictures and movies of the landscape

---

6. G. von Rad, quoted in Westermann, *Genesis 1–11*, 222.
7. Calvin, *Genesis*, 1:116, 126–27.
8. Ferguson, *Whole*, 80.

of California. At one point it seemed as though we were flying over an orange grove. There were machines that made the wind blow in the room to simulate what it would feel like to have the California breeze blowing through your hair. They even sprayed a scent into the room so you could smell the oranges. Audio played so you could hear the wind, etc. They were doing all they could to let all five of our senses drink deeply from the glories of California.

When God made the world, he had something very similar in mind. When he made the world, he filled it with many things that would show off his great goodness and glory. Mankind is supposed to regularly feel and see the sunshine, smell the rain, taste the sweetness of fruit, enjoy the coolness of water and wind, and think, "What sort of glorious and kind God made such a world for me?!" To the degree that we regularly do this, we will sin less. Meditating on truth leads to holiness. Knowing and enjoying the truth of who God is and what he has done for us and continues to do leads to obedience in daily life.

Our God is such a good God! He literally created the world to be a pleasure park for humanity. Ancient kings would have huge gardens filled with vegetation that was beautiful, aromatic, and produced tasty fruit. God built this world to be such a place for his people. He made a wonderful, beautiful world that would simultaneously show off the glory of the Creator and bring great pleasure, comfort, and joy to its inhabitants. Partially God was making it easier for humans to obey God by filling their lives with enjoyable things. He tells Adam that other than one tree he could literally eat as much as he wanted. God is so liberal, generous, lavish, and rich in his overflowing abundance!

He is the ultimate good parent. He is the best Father imaginable. In many ways Gen 2 is a parenting story. Look inside your own heart for a moment and be ruthlessly honest with yourself. Do you truly believe and fully feel the reality that our God is a good God, a wonderful loving Father, full of compassion and joy?

If you and I do not believe God is so wise and wonderful then we are already in sin. We are not loving God with all our minds in that moment, as we are commanded to do (Matt 22:37). Even if the dark fruits haven't shown much in our lives yet, the roots are there. Sin starts with false beliefs about God. What we believe about God is the most important and influential reality in our lives. By this, I do not mean what we say we believe about God. I mean what we really believe in the basement of our hearts. You might even go as far to say, what we feel to be true about God in our gut is the most important thing about us. Truth planted deeply in the soil of our soul leads to godliness in the fruit of our daily decisions.

Imagine for a moment that God had made all food and nutrients in the world to be eaten by taking one big vitamin pill. The pill is big, hard to swallow, makes you burp, and tastes bad. But that is the only way that you can get the calories you need each day to live and survive. If this were the case, we could honestly say God has provided our physical nutrients. If this were the case, it might be understandable if we only offered such a God begrudging obedience at best.

But this is not the case; far from it! Think about food. God made food beautiful to look at. It often smells wonderful. And it tastes delicious. It tastes so good that many of us now struggle with the sin of gluttony. God is such a good, wonderful, lavish Creator! He loves and delights in giving beautiful gifts to all his creatures. What sort of God must he be?!

But wait, it gets better. Right now, we are only talking about eating apples and such. Genesis 2:18–25 is one of my favorite passages in the whole Bible. Adam didn't complain that he lacked a wife. Rather, God the Father paid attention to the fact that Adam was alone. Think about it. God could have said, "Adam has food, water, beauty, nice weather, plenty of animals to play with, and most important, he has me! He can have a twenty-four-hour-a-day worship service! What more could he want or need?"

That's not what God said. God said, "It is not good for the man to be alone" (Gen 2:18). God wanted the best for Adam. God knew Adam needed a friend, a best friend at that. God knew Adam needed a lover, a wife, a companion, a helper. It makes me think about Abraham dying but before he does, he is working to make sure Isaac will have a godly wife. See Gen 24:1–4 for that story.

Some of the most enjoyable gifts of God to humanity are love, passion, romance, sex, pleasure. I could go on and get more specific, but I will stop there. All the great things we love about marriage from best friendship to making love, God invented. He is not surprised or embarrassed by these things. He gave them to his people to be enjoyed in the right times and ways. When we even think of these gifts, we should be moved to awe at such a Creator and God. What a shockingly good Father we have!

We should be simultaneously humble, happy, and holy. Genesis 2:25 tells us Adam and Eve "were both naked and were not ashamed." They were free, happy, vulnerable, innocent, trusting, and provided for. They were comfortable in their own skin. They had nothing to hide, nothing to fake, and nothing to fear. They were in paradise. We know the story doesn't end here though. They didn't live happily ever after at that point. Why?

They weren't thankful enough. Romans 1 in some ways is likely Paul's meditation on Gen 2–3. "For even though they knew God, they did not honor Him as God, or give thanks" (Rom 1:21). Matthew Henry states, "Insensibleness of God's mercies is at the bottom of our sinful departures from Him."[9]

APPLICATION

Let's talk a little more about sexuality. One of God's greatest gifts that humans have used and abused so much is the gift of sex. It is not the only sin. It is not the main sin or the worst sin and yet it is a deadly sin and one that is so prevalent. Think of all the pain in our society today that flows from sexual sin. Just think of divorce and abortion and pornography and prostitution and sexual slavery. And there's much more we could discuss.

You may be reading this and honestly think that you don't struggle with any sexual sin. You may be right. Maybe your struggles are in different areas. But I bet you know someone who struggles with sexual sin. I'll bet you've probably been impacted by it in some ways. Our culture is certainly cracking under the pressure of the consequences of our evil choices right now.

Ephesians 5:1–4 speaks powerfully to these sins. Verses 1–2 set the context. We are to imitate God, more specifically Christ. Christ loved us. Because he did, he sacrificed himself for us at the cross to save us. His life or loving sacrifice was honoring and pleasing to God. So, we too, should seek to live lives that honor and please God the Father, by imitating Christ in his sacrificial love.

There are lots of ways to love sacrificially. Verse 3 tells us that two of the main ways to do this have to do with how we use our sexuality and how we use our money. But let's focus on sex for now. Paul tells us there should be no immorality, no sexual sin. Most Christians are aware of this, but v. 4 goes further. "There must be no filthiness and silly talk, or coarse jesting, which are not fitting, but rather giving of thanks" (Eph 5:4). Paul says it's not enough to stay away from actual physical acts of sexual sin. Don't even talk about it, much less joke about it. Is this too extreme? Is this too puritanical?

---

9. Henry, *Commentary*, 564.

This does not mean all jokes about sex are wrong. Most married couples will realize that a sense of humor is necessary for a good sex life. Things don't always go according to plans. If you take your sex life too seriously you will end up idolizing it and thus probably often angry and/or disappointed. Being able to laugh at yourself and even with your spouse in healthy and loving ways is appropriate. C. S. Lewis has written helpfully on this point in *The Four Loves*: "We have reached the stage at which nothing is more needed than a roar of old-fashioned laughter.... Sensible lovers laugh."[10]

What is it that Paul is forbidding in Eph 5:4? He is forbidding Christians to treat sex like too small and insignificant of a thing. The world then and now is filled with crass and tasteless and seemingly endless sexual innuendo. Paul is saying when we think about sex, there ought to be a huge feeling of gratitude in our hearts to God over such an amazing and wonderful gift. If we thought about sex as one of God's greatest gifts, we wouldn't talk about it in such low, ugly, and dirty ways. It's not that we would always have to speak of it in a somber or clinical way either. Go read Song of Solomon! Rather, we would speak of sex in a joyful, thankful, delightful, enjoying, and God honoring way.

Some of you may think this chapter has turned into Christian sexual education. What's the point of all this? Holiness grows best in a heart of gratitude. Christian virtues blossom most in the fertile soil of thanksgiving.

The ancient Greco-Roman world was filled with all sorts of evil sexual vices and perversion. Our modern world is just as bad in some ways, if not worse. Think of all the rape, homosexuality, transgenderism, and other sins that go along with sexual sin today. Paul's words to the church coming out of such cultures then and now is to lay aside not just sinful deeds but even thoughts and words about sex that are sinful.

If the lost world hears Christians speak about sex and thinks the sum of our message is "Stop it! That's bad" we're probably not going to get far. History proves this. But that's not what Paul and the Holy Spirit say in Ephesians. They remind us of a relationship. Sex is properly thought of, spoken of, and practiced in a relationship. And I'm not primarily talking about marriage.

I'm talking about our relationship with God who made all things good for his people to enjoy. "Every perfect gift is from above, coming

---

10. Lewis, *Inspirational Writings*, 265–66.

down from the Father of lights" (Jas 1:17). If every time we thought of or spoke of sex we remembered it as an enjoyable gift invented by God for people's pleasure, I wonder how that would change out words and actions?

Whatever we do, whether we eat, drink, have sex, handle money, or whatever, we are to do it for the glory of God (see 1 Cor 10:31). We are to live all our life before his face and for his honor and glory and pleasure. We are to trust him like a good kid trusts a great, loving daddy. And we are to obey him even when we don't understand or like the command or feel like it's easy or natural.

Obedience is hard this side of Eden. Obedience is tough when sin dwells within. Obedience seems impossible while we are swimming in such a sinful culture. But obedience is progressively possible with the power of the Holy Spirit within.

One of the main weapons to fight against sin is thankfulness. What if Christians literally walked around every day in a sense of shock and awe at how good God is? What if every morning as we rolled out of bed and read God's word, we were struck afresh with how amazing God's gifts are? What if one thing on the front lobe of the minds of Christian men and women daily was what an amazing gift sex is? If when we thought of marriage, friendship, romance, passion, and intimacy we thought of a wise and good Father preparing perfect gifts for his kids, I wonder what that would do to the power of sexual temptation? I do not think it would take it all away. I do think it would greatly lessen its power in our lives.

If you struggle with sexual sin, think about praying this way each morning: "Father, you're so wise and good and loving! Thanks for inventing friendship, marriage, and sex. You are mind-blowing! Please keep me humble, happy, and grateful. Lord, make me a good, patient, self-controlled, and thankful child today. Help me steward these gifts only in the times and ways that please and honor you, so that you'll get pleasure from my life, and I'll get pleasure from your gifts!"

You could easily pray a similar prayer for whatever you struggle with. Be thankful for money and possessions if you struggle with greed. Be grateful for influence and a job and a reputation if you struggle with envy or idolizing power, etc.

We don't know for sure how long Adam lived in holiness before he fell into sin in the garden. We do know that part of what kept him in a state of holy living was a heart of gratitude. Genesis 2:23 tells us Adam's response to God's gift of Eve. It is not a stoic acknowledgment: "Oh well, I guess she's a little better than hanging out with a chimpanzee."

The language is poetic. It is the first recorded words of humanity, and it was likely a poem or song of rejoicing. It could be translated, "At last! Finally!" There is a sense in which Adam declares, "This is what I've really wanted!" The joy is overflowing.

To truly be holy, we must enjoy God and enjoy his gifts. If we aren't enjoying him and his gifts, we don't really know him well at all. The more deeply and fully we understand God, the more we will delight in him and delight to obey.

CONCLUSION

True holiness starts with truths we believe about God, ourselves, and all of life. Sinfulness starts when we don't believe the right things about God, ourselves, and all of life. We've mainly looked at life before sin today. We now live east of Eden. We are fallen. Sin lives in us. We are in a broken world where much of our experience of God's good gifts comes to us in a broken and painful way. Much hardship surrounds even the best life, the best marriage, the greatest friendships.

Hebrews 11:6 is still true though. "And without faith it is impossible to please Him, for he who comes to God must believe that He is, and that He is a rewarder of those who seek Him." True faith believes God is real and that he loves to reward people who seek him. Are you living that way? None of us do perfectly. But is this the overall tenor of your heart?

But there was one who lived his whole life in this type of faith. Hebrews 12:2–3 speaks of Christ, "who for the joy set before Him endured the cross, despising the shame, and has sat down at the right hand of the throne of God. For consider Him who has endured such hostility by sinners against Himself so that you may not grow weary and lose heart." The author of Hebrews directs us to think about Jesus. We are to direct our mental energy and focus to Christ and the cross so that when we are tempted, we can remain strong. Christ walked this earth as a real human being. He faced the same temptations that we do at the root level. And yet he passed every test ordained for him. The greatest test of his faith came as he hung alone on the cross, feeling abandoned by his good Father. He knew the truth of the goodness and generosity of God. But he experienced none of it at that moment.

His circumstances screamed at him that he was alone, forgotten, abandoned, and not provided for. But he remained faithful. He trusted. He meditated on God's word. He prayed.

We will face many dark, dangerous, and trying days where it is not easy to trust, it's hard to obey, and it seems impossible to enjoy anything from God. But look to Christ. If we are one of his people, then he literally suffered hell on earth for us on the cross. He took the eternal death that you and I merit again and again every day. When I trust in him for salvation, his life and death become the guarantee that though I may suffer temporally in this life, I'll never suffer eternally. I may feel abandoned and not provided for by my Father, but in Christ I literally already possess every spiritual blessing in the heavenly realms (Eph 1:3).

True holiness consists of trusting, obeying, and enjoying. There are sometimes in life when it's easy to trust, easy to obey, and easy to enjoy God's good gifts. There are many other times when it seems virtually impossible because life is so hard, painful, and dark. But in those days, live by faith. Cast the eyes of your mind back to Calvary. Remember the great work God has done there to free you eternally from sin. Trust in the finished work of the cross. Obey him by meditating on the power of resurrection. Enjoy all that God has done and is doing for you in Christ, by faith. And then, by his grace, seek to move forward in daily obedience in all you do for his glory.

Chapter 2

Sin Starts with Satan

Genesis 3:1–6

Human holiness and happiness start with God. Human sin starts with Satan. Genesis 2–3 makes clear that Adam and Eve were sinless until Satan arrived with lies, accusations, and temptations that led them into sin. God made Adam and Eve innocent, pure, and without shame in the garden of Eden, but they did not stay that way long. It is possible the first day Adam and Eve were alive that Satan entered the garden to tempt them.[1] This chapter will focus on the nature of the temptation we face today. We will highlight Satan's role in our temptations. For that reason, we start with a brief biblical overview of who Satan is.

The Bible does not give us a clear account of how Satan fell into sin (though there are probable allusions to it in Isa 14, Ezek 28, and the book of Revelation).[2] Ferguson says, "Some unimaginable rebellion appears to have taken place in the kingdom of heaven before the Fall of man. More than that we probably cannot say. More than that we do not require to know."[3] The Bible does give us a more detailed account of how humans originally fell into sin. This is where we should focus more of our time and energy. Understanding Gen 3 is crucial for knowing how to fight your sin today.

C. S. Lewis has wisely said, "There are two equal and opposite errors into which our race can fall about devils. One is to disbelieve their existence. The other is to believe, and to feel an excessive and unhealthy

---

1. For more on this see Fisher, *Marrow of Modern Divinity*, 67.
2. For more on this see Howard, *Exorcism*.
3. Ferguson, *Christian Life*, 140.

interest in them. They themselves are equally pleased by both errors, and hail a materialist or a magician with the same delight."[4] We don't want to give Satan too much credit or press time. Nor do we want to ignore him. We take him too lightly to our detriment.

Understanding what we realistically can about Satan's origins helps us understand him, his goals, and his attacks on our lives. Revelation 12:9 makes clear that the serpent in the garden is Satan himself lest we be confused. (Luther and Calvin believed Satan inhabited the serpent.)[5] Richard Lovelace helpfully summarizes a crucial point for us. "The Revelation of John strips away the surface of history to display the demonic force opposing the church as a dragon pursuing the bride of Christ into the wilderness, attempting to drown her in a river of lies poured out of his mouth (Rev. 12:1–17)."[6] Just because we can't see and hear a serpent speaking to us with our physical senses does not mean he is not active in our life. (I do not mean that Satan is personally pursuing you as you read this chapter. But Satan has a host of demonic entities like him to do his bidding across the planet. We ignore them at our own peril.)

Satan was made good but fell into sin. He was not content to stay in his sin alone. He hates God. His desire is to do as much damage to God as possible. God is untouchable. So, Satan seeks to attack those whom God loves. He's got thousands of years of practice at this point. He is incredibly effective.

Nothing in the Bible nor in this book is written to make us feel better about our sin. The goal of this chapter is not to say, "Satan made me do it!" This book is not meant to be the foundation of a life of blame shifting whereby we can shirk our responsibility. Far from it. But if we seek to see and slay the roots of sin at the deepest levels, we must be clear about where and how they started.

The goal of this chapter is to help us understand the role Satan plays in our daily fight with sin. His lies, accusations, and temptations are the foundations of our sin then and now. He will be fully and finally defeated one day soon. Revelation promises and predicts that. But today he is quite active. It would be wrong to say that he is alive and well. He has been severely wounded. He is bleeding out so to say. But he is an insanely savage foe, bound and determined, literally hell-bent on taking down as many people as he can with him. He is evil incarnate. Be warned.

4. Lewis, *Screwtape Letters*, 3.
5. Howard, *Exorcism*, 54.
6. Lovelace, *Dynamics*, 255.

One goal of this chapter and book is to sober us up to the dangerous world we live in. Yes, it was made wonderful and good by God as we saw in chapter 1. But now it is a war zone. It is a war zone because Satan is still so active in the world today.

During World War II Germany occupied France for over four years. In 1944 the Allied armies landed on the northern French beaches of Normandy and began to liberate France and other occupied countries. But it was almost another entire year before Germany finally and fully surrendered and the war was completely over.

Sanctification in our life is like occupied France during WWII after the Allied invasion of Normandy. The Allied forces have landed on the beach. They are steadily driving back the evil Nazis. And yet a terrible battle rages. Many lives are lost. Much destruction still occurs. The final experience of victory is sure for God's people. The timing is very unclear.

Adam and Eve lived in the garden. They had no indwelling sin. They had no surrounding sinful culture. Yet they fell because of Satan's insinuated thoughts.

We have it much worse. Sin lives inside us, though it is dying slowly. The mature Paul wrote Rom 7:14–25. He was an apostle. He had been a believer for many years. He talks about his ongoing battle with sin and temptation. If it was true of him, it is certainly true for you and me. We often do what we hate. We also often fail to do what we promise. We often stumble in sin.

Not only that, but we live immersed in a sinful culture. There is a sinful culture in all the world ruled by Satan, "the prince of the power of the air" (Eph 2:2). Not all things in culture are evil. There is much good in it that reflects the Creator. And yet it is all tainted by sinful influences.

The deck seems stacked against us in some respects. Sin lives in us. Satan lives outside of us. Sin also surrounds us in the world's culture. We must be sober minded. If Satan could tempt Adam and Eve effectively into sin in such a paradise, how much more likely is he to win the battle against us in the day-to-day fight against sin?

Listen to several great theologians as to how Satan is able to influence believers. "The Devil trades in false statements.... How insidiously he infers in the conscience of God's children that their Savior is 'not really' all that he is made out to be. It is better, wiser, safer, suggests the Devil, not to trust Christ too far.... There can be no doubt that some of the of the irrational fears, doubts and thoughts which Christians experience should be traced back to the ambush in which Satan hides."[7] Thomas Watson teaches, based on Eph 6:16 that temptation is a dart Satan can inject into the minds of believers. He says, "When evil thoughts are thrown into the mind, when we loathe and have reluctance to them[,] . . . Satan has injected these impure emotions."[8]

Thomas Brooks shows that Satan casts vain thoughts into our souls. He goes further: "They pass through the best hearts, they are lodged and cherished only in the worst hearts."[9] Finally, John Calvin teaches us that Satan seeks "to divert us from the simplicity with which we should serve God and our neighbor" through thoughts that we imagine.[10]

"Whatever is not from faith is sin" (Rom 14:23). Remember the previous chapter. Holiness starts with faith, trusting God. Thus, all sin starts with doubting God. The deepest root of all sin is unbelief. "Without faith it is impossible to please" God (Heb 11:6).

Satan came into the garden bringing much doubt in tow. God had clearly commanded the humans to avoid one certain tree in the garden called "the tree of the knowledge of good and evil" (Gen 2:17). Satan came and sought to reverse that command. We don't know for sure but this likely happened the very first day Adam and Eve lived together in the garden. He tempts them and us, now and then, to doubt God's word, God's wrath, and God's ways.

DOUBTING GOD'S WORD

Satan is crafty and shrewd. Being crafty and shrewd is a good thing when used in the service of God. In Matt 10:16 Jesus commands his people to be as shrewd as a serpent (likely referring to this passage) while also maintaining the innocence of a dove. Satan used his shrewdness to rebel and serve his own means. We often do this today and for this we must repent.

So much of Satan's shrewdness is in his subtlety, his seeming smallness. His words in Gen 3 seem small and light at first glance. They are rarely direct lies. They are little insinuations. Like the theme of the great Christopher Nolan movie *Inception*, he is planting ideas in the minds of the first humans, which will later come to full fruition. The movie is

---

7. Ferguson, *Life*, 140.
8. Watson, *Lord's Prayer*, 261, quoted in Ferguson, *Life*, 142.
9. Brooks, *Precious*, 137.
10. Calvin, *2 Samuel*, 450.

in the science fiction genre. In the movie people find ways to enter the minds of others and plant a small idea that can later blossom into actual life decisions and patterns in the real world. Satan does the same thing to us. He can influence our thinking in ways that can affect our lives. Satan came to Adam and Eve with a glancing blow, but it was, oh, so effective.

He throws a tiny pebble of doubt into the river of their minds, and it starts a ripple effect that will ruin the universe. The ripple continues today. It lives in your heart, soul, and mind and in mine as well. He did not come in power with thunder, lightning, fear, and terror. He came as a seeming friend, a sage, an advisor of sorts, maybe even a counselor.

He came with a seemingly innocent observation and question. He deceived them and he still deceives us with mere thoughts, words, ideas, suggestions, and thought patterns. In Gen 3:1 it is as though he says, "Hey guys, nice to meet you. Did I hear correctly that God said you had to work in this garden all day long, but you're never permitted to eat the fruit of your own labor? Surely that's not right, is it? All these trees are prohibited for you guys?!"

Now, this assertion is obviously untrue. But Derek Kidner, the great Old Testament commentator, wisely points out that Satan's question "smuggles in the assumption that God's word is subject to our judgement."[11] And human beings have been questioning God's word ever since.

This doubt about God's word is where sin starts. When we start to think we have a right to decide whether to obey we are already in trouble. When we start to say to ourselves, "Well, if I can't fully understand this text, then I'm not sure I'm going to obey the clear implications of the verse" we are already in sin. This isn't living by faith. This isn't the holiness we discussed in chapter 1 that starts with trusting. Another Old Testament scholar states "the essence of sin is to put human judgement above divine command."[12]

But it's worse than that. It's not just an attack on God's word. It is an attack on his character. Satan is trying to magnify "God's strictness."[13] And it worked. And it still works today, doesn't it?

Satan tells us that God gives his law to squish our fun and keep us from our full potential. Satan portrays God not as a loving Father but as a tyrant, hell bent on being strict and stingy with our enjoyment of the human experience. These lies have sunk so deep in the collective human

11. Kidner, *Genesis*, 67.
12. Wenham, "Genesis," 63.
13. Kidner, *Genesis*, 68.

consciousness. The truth is that God's law directs us how best to enjoy the human experience fully.

Think of how these powerful lies still impact the world today. Did God really say . . .? Does the Bible really teach there were miracles like the flood and the Red Sea separating and the resurrection of Christ? Are we sure?

"I don't know," someone might say. "That sounds weird to me. I'm not sure I can really believe this book you call the Bible." Please listen to me. There is a humble and honest way to wrestle with God's word because so often it is so marvelous that it is hard to believe. The greatest example may come in Luke 1:34. An angelic being has just told a normal teenage girl she's about to be pregnant. She's not superstitious. She's not even a little "stitious." She asks what any woman in such a situation, in any day and age might ask, "How can this be, since I am a virgin?" God is pleased when we express our honest questions and concerns about his word in a humble way that is ready to believe and wants to trust him because we do trust his character and track record.

But there is also an arrogant way to question God. We can be condescending and faithless in a doubtful way. The same angel shows up in the same chapter a little earlier to speak with a priest named Zacharias. Zach is told his wife is going to have a baby as well. He basically says, "How can I be sure this is true? My wife is old and barren and past childbearing age anyway" (see Luke 1:7, 13–20). Gabriel the angel is not happy. He basically says, "Oh, you want a sign, do you? I'll give you a sign. You'll be mute, unable to speak, until the child is born."

To question in arrogance and "know-it-all-ism" never ends well. To question humbly, with a desire for more understanding and faith rewarded. How do you approach God's word?

Now let's give Eve her due. At first, she responds well. She essentially quotes God's word, which is the right way to attack doubt and temptation. She seems to win round one.

But we must also give Satan his due. He is incredibly persevering. He is not easily dissuaded. He does not give up so easily. Thousands of years later Satan tempted Jesus and lost three times. Luke 4:13 tells us that he eventually left. But he did not leave for good. He left "until an opportune time." Satan is an expert in knowing when we are weak, when our guard is down, and attacking us relentlessly during those times. In the garden, he sensed the time was right. He smelled doubt in the air and so he progressed to his second attack.

DOUBTING GOD'S WRATH

Now, in the first temptation to doubt, did you notice, Satan didn't directly tell a lie. He asked a question. He created the opportunity for us to infer, develop, and adopt a lie he insinuated. How subtle, how crafty, how shrewd. He feigned ignorance. He planted a thought. Partially he wanted to muddy the water, to make things obscure and cloudy and uncertain. This is one of his methods. God speaks clearly and precisely. Satan seeks to make it as confusing and complicated as possible. He still does this today.

I've talked to so many college students who claim to be Christians and understand theology very well. But when it comes to what the Bible says about sleeping with their girlfriend, suddenly, they seem to get very unclear. They become experts at taking incredibly basic and clear passages with obvious meaning and twisting them into confusion and cloudiness. Surely Satan is behind this.

This problem doesn't just affect college students. It's striking how it affects us all. Even those of us who are biblically informed and theologically astute struggle to see Scripture's plan when it's teaching about something we care deeply about. We all have blind spots to certain biblical teachings. Even when the Bible is totally clear, we might think, it could not mean that . . . because we wish it meant something else. Whether we doubt the biblical mandate on sacrificial financial giving or the responsibility to visit orphans, widows, and prisoners in distress, most of us have at least one place where we intentionally soften the Bible's commands to us personally. Satan's work continues to thrive today.

Satan seems bolder with the second temptation. Yet, some would say this second temptation is not necessarily an outright lie. In Gen 3:4 he exclaims, "You surely shall not die!" It is more of a half truth. If you know the story, you know Adam and Eve will eventually sin. But they do not fall dead in the garden. In fact, they go on to live for hundreds of years. Did Satan know this was true? Did he speak from personal experience? He had rebelled against God in time past and yet he lived on. Would the same not be true for humans as well? He doesn't know for sure but maybe; he proceeds on a hunch.

He insinuates that God is merciful and so they can and should abuse his mercy. There will be some consequences, but they can't be all that bad. The juice is worth the squeeze. Eat the forbidden fruit!

With this line of reasoning, he plants a further doubt in Eve's mind about the seriousness of God's word. How trustworthy is God's word? Is it mostly true but occasionally a little exaggerated? Can you play loosey goosey with his threats? Satan seems to think so.

This time his doubt is directed at God's wrath, his power, his consequences, his seriousness. "Maybe God said you will die, but he's speaking in hyperbole. It's an overstatement. Don't get all worked up about it! Relax."

Some of you may become bored with this ancient history and the story of a talking snake. But is not this same doubt alive and well in the world today? Does it not even thrive in the church in many corners?

Have you ever heard someone say (or maybe you've said or thought yourself), "I know the Bible is clear on hell, but I just don't get it. I have a tough time with that. Does God really mean that he will punish rebels for all eternity? Surely that can't be right! How could a loving God do such a thing?! I don't think I can believe in such a God." The old lie is alive and well.

"Maybe hell really refers to annihilation. Maybe hell is a metaphor for the painful consequences of sin in this life?" I have seen well-meaning Christians follow this type of logic. The most mature will admit that, when they start to doubt the reality of eternal hell, it has nothing to do with Bible study and exegesis. Rather, it has to do with emotions about right, wrong, and their personal notion of justice. Be careful. We can all fall into this pattern.

The sin underneath the sin in this example is that we subtly imagine we are smarter than God. We would never say that out loud, but our thought patterns betray our true beliefs. If we read clear biblical teaching and think, "Surely, that's not so! We know better than that now," we have already fallen into Satan's scheme.

Doubting hell is one modern example. There are many more. It's not hard to see how slippery the slope is. If I throw out one clear biblical doctrine because it offends me, what's to say I won't throw out the next one that bothers me as well? At this point Eve has not fallen. But it does seem that she is tottering. She doesn't respond. Satan senses he has the advantage and goes for the kill. He has no mercy. Beware that we do not fall into the same or a similar scheme.

DOUBTING GOD'S WAYS

Now Satan really attacks the character of God. He attacks God's love and goodness. It is still not an outright lie. There is an element of truth in it. Their eyes will be opened in a sense. They will have a new knowledge of evil and of the difference between good and evil. "In the day you eat from it your eyes will be opened, and you will be like God, knowing good and evil" (Gen 3:5).

This statement of Satan in v. 5 is the one that pushed Adam and Eve over the edge. The implication is simply that God is not good. He is not trustworthy. "God does not have your best in mind. He may give you some good stuff, but he will never give you the best stuff! He will hold you down. He will keep you back from life's greatest thrills! Don't trust him! Rather, compete with him. Become him! Rise up, like I did. Take his place."

Satan insinuated ever so slightly that God is not a good Father. He wants us to think and feel "God does not have our best in mind. He is an evil task master demanding we work slave labor in his world without letting us eat all the fruit of our labor. It's not fair! It's not right! We shouldn't stand for it. He is a tyrant, a selfish landowner."

Satan implies, "God is taking advantage of you. He's using you. You can't trust him! You must stand up for yourself and demand your rights! Seize the day! Think for yourself! Take the fruit!"

Derek Kidner says it "is a lie big enough to reinterpret life . . . and dynamic enough to redirect the flow of affection and ambition."[14] The energy God had given humanity to love, pursue, and obey him now flows against him. The warmth and affection we had in his embrace is now turned into a cold shoulder of suspicion.

Sinclair Ferguson has spoken at length on this important event. This is a long quote but so helpful. Please read it slowly and carefully:

> The lie by which the Serpent deceived Eve was enshrined in the double suggestion that
>
> 1) this Father was in fact restrictive, self-absorbed, and selfish since he would not let them eat from any of the trees, and
>
> 2) his promise of death if they were disobedient was simply false.
>
> Thus the lie was an assault on both God's generosity and his integrity. . . . This, in fact, is the lie that sinners have believed ever since—the lie of the not-to-be-trusted-because-he-does-not-love-me-false-Father. . . . What was injected into Eve's mind and affections . . . was a deep-seated suspicion of God . . . dulling her senses, and destroying her affection for her heavenly Father. . . . For what the Serpent accomplished in Eve's mind,

---

14. Kidner, *Genesis*, 68.

affections, and will was a divorce between God's revealed will and his gracious, generous character. . . . It is this—a failure to see the generosity of God and his wise and loving plans for our lives[,] . . . a forbidding God. . . . She was deceived into "hearing" law only as negative deprivation and not as the wisdom of a heavenly Father[,] . . . the "lie about God," that has entered the bloodstream of the human race. . . . Scratch anyone who is not a Christian, and this (whatever they may say) is their heart disposition. Any profession to the contrary is itself a further form of self-deception. . . . God becomes a magnified policeman. . . . The 'lie' that we now believe is that 'to glorify God' is not, indeed cannot be, "to enjoy him for ever," but to lose all joy. . . . How do I think about God, and what instincts and dispositions and affections toward him does this evoke in me? . . . How we feel toward God as well as the doctrine of God we profess [is crucial.] . . . [Satan] used the commandment to deceive Eve about the nature of the commandment giver. She saw only one law—the negative one—not the many blessings of God's commands. . . . Having found a landing place here in the case of Eve, Satan continues to land in the same territory in our lives too. But now he has grown from a serpent into a dragon exercising his malicious deceptive ministry. . . . He is therefore determined to destroy our enjoyment of our new relationship to the Lord. The first satanic attack had this in view and sought to disrupt the first couple's confident assurance of God's benevolence. . . . This first temptation . . . is surely also paradigmatic.[15]

Notice this is not a new age, therapeutic, mushy, extreme charismatic speaking. (No offense to doctrinally sound charismatics!) He is one of the greatest theologians alive today and part of what he emphasizes is how we "feel" about God is super important to how we will live for God and with God. Let the implications of that statement sink in for a minute. One of the main premises of this book and, I believe, the Bible is that you can have a head full of accurate knowledge that you profess to intellectually believe and yet your heart can be so cold and hard and distant from feeling the realities of those truths so that they make little to no impact on your day-to-day life!

I recently read a true story about a woman who was a professing believer who had an affair. She had grown up in church. Her father was a pastor. As she unpacked how she got into the affair she made the following statement about events from her past and how they had influenced

---

15. Ferguson, *Whole*, 68–69, 82–85, 132–33, 220.

her. "When my mom died[,] . . . I was pretty sure God didn't want me to be happy. I became a different person."[16]

Satan doesn't fight fair. He is determined to destroy our enjoyment of and belief in our wonderful, friendly heavenly Father. Satan lies to us and deceives us ever so subtly about the nature of God and of ourselves. "God isn't good and you're not all you could or should be." Most of Satan's lies contain enough truth to make them plausible. Adam and Eve weren't all they could be. They could grow. And yet, in that moment of innocence they were all they were supposed to be, all God wanted them to be in that moment.

Once we start believing Satan's words and thoughts about God and about ourselves, our whole worldview changes. How you experience much of life will change. I have a counselor friend who says our view of self and view of God are like two lenses in a pair of glasses that help us see all of life. John Calvin's *Institutes* starts on this point as well. If our view of God and self are right, our view of all other things comes into alignment eventually. To the degree that our view of God and/or self is distorted, our understanding of all reality will be impaired.

Can you see how Satan's lies from Gen 3 are still wreaking havoc on the world today. Many people today have all sorts of sexual feelings and desires inside of them that don't align with God's word. God says all people should only have sex in the context of a monogamous heterosexual marriage. And even then, you can only have sex when your spouse is willing.

What if I find homosexual desires in myself? What if my heterosexual desires rage so much I want to sleep with ten different partners? It's so easy, almost natural to doubt God's word. Did he really say that? Our desires can rage like a river overflowing its proper banks.

And sinful desires are not confined to sexuality. How many of us are often tempted to overeat? How many of us find it so hard to stop after a couple of glasses of wine? How many of us are driven to just close one more deal and make a little more money, even if that means overworking and neglecting our family? Our desires can become a never satisfied slave driver if we let them.

Practically speaking, we all doubt his word every day in some form or fashion. Each time we chose to sin we are doubting God's word in that

---

16. Key, *Stay Married*, 197.

moment, whether we know it or not. We are doubting if God's word is best for us in a certain area.

It's so easy to doubt his wrath. Did he really mean . . .? Will he really punish?

It's so easy to doubt his ways. We doubt his truth, his power, and his love and we thus suffer so much for our doubt. We must fix our eyes on our God, his truth, his wisdom, his goodness.

Much of Gen 2 and 3 refer to God as the LORD God. This is reminding us that God is Yahweh. He is the covenant making and keeping God. He is a relational God who wants to be married to his people spiritually.

But when Satan speaks of God, he refers to him merely as God. Satan is seeking to emphasize God's power, God's control, and thus leave out his goodness and love and make him appear as a tyrant. Satan whispers, "He's only the Creator. He's not caring. He's not gentle. He's not tender. He's not trustworthy."

Here is Satan's logic: "Is it really sinful or wrong? Well, maybe so. Maybe just a little. But what's the big deal?! Is it really that bad or dangerous or harmful? You're not hurting anyone, are you? Not much at least. Even if you are hurting someone a little, isn't it worth it? Sin is so fun. You may not need to do this sin, but don't you really want to? Come on, jump in, the water feels great!"

APPLICATION

Genesis 3:6 is where Eve finally gives in and so do we. The food was going to taste good and fill her stomach. It looked beautiful and alluring, as sin so often does. And it would make her wise. What could be wrong with that?!

Now, desires for satisfaction, beauty, and wisdom are obviously not wrong in and of themselves. They are good, right, and God given. But Satan is so sly and cunning because he often appeals to our good desires to lead us astray. He appeals to a good root desire but leads us to satisfy it in a sinful time and way. For example, if you are engaged to be married, it's normal, good, and right that you desire to have sex with your fiancé. It's just that the timing is not right. You must wait until your wedding. But Satan appeals to this normal, good, right desire and says, "Seize the day. Fulfill yourself now! Grab the fruit when and how you want. Don't let God hold you back!"

REMOVING REBELLION'S ROOTS

Genesis 2:9 says every tree was "pleasing to the sight." Genesis 3:6 says the tree was a "delight." Exodus 20:17 says don't "covet." Pleasing, delight, and covet all have the same root word in Hebrew.

God made trees to look good and fruit to taste good. That's not bad or wrong. But when God-given desires for good gifts become demands to have them my way, right away, we are in sin. We are coveting and breaking the tenth commandment.

Satan promised Adam and Eve "something beyond good."[17] The problem is nothing genuinely good ever exists beyond God's established good! Trust him and don't chase phantom pleasures that don't even exist!

One commentator says, "Here is the essence of covetousness. It is the attitude that says I need something I do not now have in order to be happy."[18] Doubt leads to pride. Pride leads to coveting. These are the roots of sin.

Rather than trusting, we doubt. Rather than obeying, we boast and rebel. Rather than enjoying and thanking God for all we already have, we start coveting and demanding more. The logic is of an abandoned orphan. It's the scarcity mentality. "If God isn't good and isn't going to use his power to provide all I want and need then who will provide me?!" The obvious answer quickly becomes, "I guess I must provide for myself. And if I've got to break rules to do so, then so be it!"

Tim Keller teaches that sin "begins when we assume we have the right and wisdom to even decide if we should obey. As soon as you begin asking: 'is this obedience to God really beneficial for me or not? Should I obey this or not?'—then you have already disobeyed! . . . You are assuming God's place. . . . You are already committed to the supposition that you can stand in judgment over the wisdom of God. . . . the desire to be . . . 'like God' has now passed into every human heart and informs absolutely everything we do, whether consciously or unconsciously, whether we are Christians or non-believers. . . . When the desire for anything else grows greater than the desire to please God, then we are ready to sin."[19]

In another place Keller writes,

> All sin against God is grounded in a refusal to believe that God is more dedicated to our good, and more aware of what that is than we are. We distrust God because we assume he is not truly

---

17. Kidner, *Genesis*, 69.
18. Hamilton, *Book of Genesis*, 190.
19. Keller, *What Were We Put in the World to Do?*, 43–45.

> for us, that if we give him complete control, we will be miserable. . . . "If I obey God I'll miss out! I need to be happy." That's the justification. Sin always begins with the character assassination of God. We believe that God has put us in a world of delights but has determined that he will not give them to us if we obey him. . . . This delusion has sunk deep into every human heart. One of the main reasons that we trust God too little is because we trust our own wisdom too much. . . . This is really the most fundamental temptation that there has even been in the world, and the original sin. Specific details may vary, but the deep heart song of "I have to look out for myself" is always there.[20]

Many Christians are great at seeing how the sinful culture does this. But can we honestly assess the smaller ways we do the exact same things? Consider the true believer who tends to judge himself too harshly. Every time they commit the smallest sin, they doubt their salvation. I talked to a woman today who grew up in a great Presbyterian church, in a good homeschool community, and has served overseas as a missionary. She is in full-time ministry now. But she said there was a season of her life where every time she sinned, she'd pray the "sinner's prayer" again to be sure she was really saved. Imagine the subconscious thought process behind this practice. "I know the Bible teaches once saved always saved, but does that really apply to me?" See how the tiny lie sneaks in: "God's not really that good and forgiving, is he?"

I spoke with another woman yesterday who grew up in a good Presbyterian family as well. She's about to get a divorce. I told her that she doesn't have biblical grounds because the Bible teaches you can only get a divorce if there's adultery or abandonment. She said, "I used to believe that, but now I don't." I asked her what Scripture had changed her mind. She admitted the Bible had not changed her mind but another book she'd read that explained that God's heart has changed, and he wouldn't want you to stay in a hard marriage.

How many Christian men know what Jesus clearly said about lustful looks and thoughts but honestly think and feel it's not that bad? "I'm not looking at porn. It's just a few fantasy thoughts. Who can it really hurt? I'm bored. My wife is cold. I need some excitement!"

Satan gets our mind off God's goodness and word and focused onto hardship and how we feel deprived in some way. Or he emphasizes areas of life where we feel like a victim. He seems to have done this to half of the

---

20. Keller, *Prophet*, 137–39.

United States in the last few years. Doubting God's goodness and feeling like we deserve more because we are a victim becomes one of the deepest roots of our sin.

I worked with a student years ago who was really growing spiritually. He participated in a college ministry that took overseas missions' trips but only a limited number of students could go each year. He wanted to go. He was not asked and was very hurt, bitter, and pouting. He couldn't shake it. He told me, "I feel like God owes me. I deserve to go. I didn't get what I deserve." See the logic. I didn't get what I wanted and thought was best for me. So, God must not be good. He's not fair. This lie goes all the way back to the garden.

I have another friend who waited until he was almost thirty to get married. The whole time he fought to stay sexually pure. He later said he felt like he had made a deal with God. "I'll stay pure if you'll give me a great wife." He has been married several years now, and his marriage is incredibly hard. He told me he feels like God broke his end of the deal. So, he said he feels like he and God are roommates that do not speak to one another anymore. Again, this man used to work for a ministry. He has really good intellectual theology. But see how the satanic lies run wild in his heart and feelings, despite his theology.

This student and this adult friend both had good theology. They know all we deserve is hell. They would pay lip service to that doctrine. But when push came to shove the motives and true beliefs of their hearts were revealed. They were living as though their virtuous deeds earned them a right to tell God how to run the universe. Our pride runs so deep.

In the grand scheme of things, the sin of pouting about a missed missions trip seems about as small and insignificant as it gets. But do you not see that when you dig into the significant part it's truly a strike at the heart of the gospel and the most fundamental doctrines of all?! Don't take your domesticated sin lightly.

The goal of this book is to rip the lid off the respectability of so many of our so-called small sins to see the evil lurking beneath so that we can put them to death before they grow to a level to kill us. John Owen, one of the best theologians of all time, teaches that Satan "injects evil and blasphemous thoughts into the hearts of God's saints. Satan does this directly. . . . He forges these fiery darts, with which he attacks us."[21]

---

21. Owen, *Sin and Temptation*, 100.

Do not wrongly assume that Satan cannot inject sinful thoughts into the minds of believers. Howard insightfully says, "Satan has been brought down, judged, defeated—and yet he still exercises sufficient power to the extent that Christ's prayer for his disciples is that they be kept from the evil one (John 17:15)."[22] Matthew 16:16–23 is a clear example of Satan influencing the thinking of a genuine believer who had just been affirmed by Jesus himself. "Believers are thus called to be defensively minded in spiritual matters—relentlessly on guard against satanic assault (see Acts 4:23–31; 2 Cor 11:3–4, 11:12–14; Eph 6:16, 18–20; 1 Thess 3:3; 1 Pet 5:8–9; 1 John 3:8–12), even though their victory in Christ is certain (1 John 4:1–6).[23] Satan has been doing this very effectively for thousands of years and you are not immune. Please be honest with yourself now about how these delusions are showing up in your heart today. And then be honest about how they don't seem that bad compared to what we hear on the news about the pagans we live around. But they are still exceedingly evil, and we must remember as Keller said above, they are character assassinations of God!

CONCLUSION

Almost as soon as the sin is committed God shows up on the scene. He curses Satan and part of the curse on Satan in Gen 3:15 is a promise to humanity. Humans will continue to live. They will have babies. And one day a second Adam will arise. He will walk the earth. He will battle with Satan. He will be terribly wounded. But by his wounds we are healed. With his heel he will crush Satan's head and lies forever.

Adam was already like God when Satan entered the garden. But that was not enough for him. He wanted to be more like God. He demanded it. He grasped after the forbidden fruit.

The Lord Jesus Christ was eternally with God and just like God. He was and is fully God. Yet he did not grasp on to what he already had. He didn't demand his rights and privileges but rather laid them down willingly. He laid his glorious benefits aside to be brought low to earth, to poverty, to the cross, to pain, to suffering, death, hell, and the grave. He suffered all this for all the sins of all his people for all time.

---

22. Howard, *Exorcism*, 42.
23. Howard, *Exorcism*, 37.

Sin started with us looking to ourselves with satanic wisdom to fix a problem that wasn't even real. We had no problem. We were in paradise. Now, because of our sin and stupidity, we have a problem now.

Salvation starts with Christ leaving paradise and then with us looking to him. Look to Christ alone to fully fix your real problem, your ongoing sin problem. Look at him initially the first time in salvation. Continue to stare at him with eyes of faith until you see him face to face:

> Turn your eyes upon Jesus
> Look full in His wonderful face
> And the things of earth will grow strangely dim
> In the light of His glory and grace.[24]

Christ has finally and fully solved our only ultimate problem, our sin that separates us from all the goodness of God. Trust him!

The cross is the greatest demonstration of God's truth, power, and love. God's wisdom, strength, and goodness have conspired together to save us. We should spend all our lives going deeper in trusting, obeying, and enjoying all he has for us.

---

24. Lemmel, "Turn Your Eyes upon Jesus," 335.

Chapter 3

Lies Rooted in Reality

Job 1–2

In John 8:44, Jesus says that the devil "is the father of lies." Every lie originates with Satan. Revelation 12:9 teaches that Satan "deceives the whole world." We have all been touched by his lies. No one is immune. All people living on planet earth have been and are to some degree being deceived by his lies, no matter how small and subtle they may be. You may have been walking with Christ for over eighty years now. You may be the most mature believer on planet earth with much life experience and multiple degrees in theology. Yet, until you are safe at home with Christ, you are in the battle of God's truth vs. Satan's lies. Hence the battle for holiness is a battle for truth.

All sin starts with Satan. Sin starts with lies we believe. Satan is an expert liar. He roots his lies in enough reality to make them believable. All good liars know this trick. This chapter will drill deeper into the reality we looked at in chapter two. Satan is a master liar. He did not just lie in the garden and then leave humanity alone. He continues to lie. He personalizes lies. He works hard to make the circumstances of each of our lives seemingly "speak" a lie to us. He used the circumstances of the garden to help give plausibility to his lies to Adam and Eve. Likewise, he uses the circumstances of each of our lives to give plausibility to his ongoing lies. The goal of this chapter is to expose the deepest roots of the lies we believe and the sins we commit.

Imagine that you like to smoke cigarettes, but a spouse or parent has begged you to stop. You say OK but continue to smoke. One night you come home from smoking with friends. A family member asks if you have been smoking. You respond, "No, but all my friends were and that's why I smell this way." You have lied. But you bathed your lie in enough truth to make it very plausible. It is 100 percent true that your friends were smoking. It is mostly true that a large reason your clothes smell like smoke is the result of your friends smoking. It minimizes and hides the fact that you were also smoking. It is a lie surrounded by truth and this is much easier to convince others to believe. In similar ways Satan does the same things to us. He is an expert strategist when it comes to making his deceptions seem so realistic.

God had called the forbidden tree "the tree of the knowledge of good and evil" in Gen 2:17. In Gen 3 Satan seemed to use God's name for the tree to enhance his temptation to Eve. "See the tree is called the tree of the knowledge of good and evil. So, it must make you wiser. It must give you more knowledge about good and about evil. It must give you knowledge you don't now have."

Matthew Henry wisely states, "To support this part of the temptation, he abuses the name given to this tree: he perverts the sense of it, as if this tree would give them a speculative notional knowledge of the natures, kinds, and originals, of good and evil."[1] The real battle against sin is in our minds. Second Corinthians 10:3 and 5 say, "We do not wage war according to the flesh. . . . We are destroying speculations and every lofty thing raised up against the knowledge of God, and we are taking every thought captive to the obedience of Christ." Spiritual warfare is about speculations, knowledge, and thoughts. It's a battle between believing the truth or lies. Hence, the battle for holiness is a battle for truth. Satan is an expert in his craft with thousands of years of warfare under his belt. He roots his lies in enough truth to make them quite easy for you and me to swallow them whole.

There was truth in the statement that they would know about good and evil from eating this tree. They would experience evil in themselves and see its horrible effects. They would have more knowledge, but it would be terrible. It would be like a doctor learning more about a deadly disease not through academic research but through catching the painful disease itself.

Dallas Willard says, "Ideas [are] a primary stronghold of evil in the human self and in society."[2] John Mark Comer, a pastor and writer on the

1. Henry, *Commentary*, 9.
2. Willard, *Renovation*, 99, quoted in Comer, *Live*, 36.

West Coast of the US, agrees. "All temptation [is] the appeal to believe a lie, to believe an illusion about reality. . . . The devil's primary stratagem . . . is deceptive ideas that play to disordered desires, which are normalized in a sinful society. . . . The devil's lies aren't random untrue facts with no emotional value."[3]

When my sons were younger one made fun of the other for having a large forehead. I don't think it was true. It was a lie. But it was a little humorous to me because in the grand scheme of things, who cares if your forehead is slightly larger than someone else's? If Satan were to whisper in my mind that my forehead was large, I think I would shrug and say, "Who cares?" But to my younger son, the lie hurt. He looked up to his older brother. He cared deeply about his older brother's opinion. If his older brother thought something was wrong with the shape of his head, it stung him. Satan will find ways to lie to each of us that will sting and stick with us. The lie he may tell me may seem laughable to you. But to me, Satan will be shrewd enough to ensure that something about my circumstances makes it seem true and terribly painful.

Comer is so helpful in showing us that Satan will find ways to lie to us in ways that appeal to us emotionally. Adam and Eve wanted knowledge. That's a good desire. He appealed to a good desire to lure them into sin. And he does the exact same thing to us today. Beware for how Satan seeks to personalize lies in your life to appeal to your good desires. He will start with a good desire and then take you on a roller coaster of sin with many painful turns and twists.

Think of how Eve must have felt in the garden that day. "Where did this talking snake come from? I've never heard of talking snakes. No one told me about him. I must lack more knowledge than I thought. And this snake seems wise. He has knowledge I don't have. Maybe Adam didn't know about the talking snake? Maybe Adam lacks knowledge too? God has been holding out on us!"

How does this same pattern play out in our lives—in our day, when a talking snake in a garden is not what we face? Satan today uses subtltey much more effectively than coming as a literal speaking snake. If a snake came and started to speak to us our guard would be up! But when we are just experiencing normal life, Satan is often easily able to sneak past our defenses.

---

3. Comer, *Live*, 57, 59.

Many secular writers have written about unwanted intrusive thoughts. Eckhart Tolle, a German spiritualist, wrote in 1997 that people are controlled by "compulsive[,] . . . involuntary thought processes[,] . . . continuous monologues or dialogues." An involuntary thought process "comments, speculates, judges, compares, complains, likes, dislikes. . . . I would say about 80 to 90 percent of most people's thinking is not only repetitive and useless but, because of its dysfunctional and often negative nature, much of it is also harmful."[4] Anne Lamott has similarly written, "In your head twenty-four hours a day, nonstop in stereo. Out of the right speaker in your inner ear will come the endless stream of self-aggrandizement, the recitation of one's specialness. . . . Out of the left speaker will be the rap songs of self-loathing, the lists of all the things one doesn't do well."[5] Jordan Peterson summarizes Sigmund Freud, "We are not the masters of our own houses. . . . We're more like haunted houses filled with autonomous spirits." Peterson says that Carl Jung "made the case that we are haunted by demons and gods."[6] This experience of intrusive thoughts is universal to humanity.

Some of us may think, "Well that may be true for non-Christians, but certainly not for believers." But again, we must listen to wise Bible teachers that show us how even believers can be taken captive by Satan's evil thought processes. Ferguson teaches it is very hard to distinguish between when Satan speaks to us and when our heart is speaking to us. "The enemies we face attack us from outside our own hearts and move inward with insistent force to draw our affections towards themselves and away from our Lord Jesus Christ. But their power rests on a further factor, namely the 'landing ground' they are able to find within our own lives. . . . There is still, in the Christian, a base of operations from which Satan is able to work, an enemy within." Thomas Watson teaches that Satan suddenly injected a motion into King David who was definitely a believer.[7] Thomas Brooks shows that sometimes what we think to be our own opinions or even "the inspirations of God . . . are the whisperings and hissings of that serpent."[8]

---

4. Eckhart Tolle, quoted in Andrée Seu Peterson, "Poisonous Thoughts," 70.
5. Anne Lamott, quoted in Andrée Seu Peterson, "Poisonous Thoughts," 70.
6. Jordan Peterson, quoted in Andrée Seu Peterson, "Poisonous Thoughts," 70.
7. Ferguson, *Life*, 142–43, 145.
8. Brooks, *Precious*, 28.

Calvin goes as far to say of David, in speaking of his murdering Uriah, that the "devil has taken such possession of him."[9] He further teaches "how subtle the devil is. He pops in as soon as he finds a breach, just waiting for the door to be opened. Indeed, he knows how to enter without being invited, just asking for a little crack. . . . What will happen when we voluntarily cast ourselves into Satan's nets?"[10] These truths should sober us all.

The story of Job is extremely helpful in this regard. The story of Job is much more relatable. There is a normal man, with a wife, kids, servants, businesses, animals, dealing with weather, trauma, friends, and heartache. Much of it seems very much like our lives. And yet the same pattern emerges.

It is likely that Job and Genesis were the first two books of the Bible written down. It is interesting that Satan is a main character in the first two to three chapters of each book. What is God trying to tell us about how crucial and foundational it is for all people to understand this nature of spiritual warfare? It affects all our lives whether we realize it or not.

Part of what is so helpful about the first two chapters of Job is that we see two scenes playing out, side by side. We get an up close and personal view of what happened to Job on planet earth. But simultaneously we get to go behind the curtain and see what was really happening with God and Satan in the spiritual realms.

SATAN WANTS

In Job 1:6–11 Satan tells God that the only reason Job serves God is because of God's gifts and blessings. If all of these are removed, Job will hate God and curse him to his face. That is Satan's proposal. He likely truly believes it.

Satan's ultimate desire and goal is for people everywhere to curse God. God wants people around the globe to love, trust, obey, and praise him. Satan wants the opposite.

Satan does not care whether we curse God out loud with our mouths or just with our decisions and lifestyle decisions. The result is the same. Satan wants to do all he can to drive a wedge between people and their

---

9. Calvin, *Sermons*, 510.
10. Calvin, *Sermons*, 624–25.

Creator. He wants to convince us that God does not love us. That's what he did with Adam and Eve. It's what he wants to do with us.

John Knox, the father of Scottish Presbyterians teaches, "By what means Satan first drew mankind from the obedience of God the Scripture doth witness. Namely, by pouring into their hearts that poison—that God did not love them; and by affirming that by transgression of God's commandments they might attain to felicity and joy; so that he caused them to seek life where God had pronounced death to be."[11] The original set of lies Satan told Adam and Eve has infected all humans ever since save one. This lie forms a landing ground or a beach head in all our hearts for Satan to deepen our feeling that this lie is true, that God does not love us. We will see Satan trying to grow and exploit this lie in Job's heart through the circumstances he experienced. Satan uses all the power and influence he has to deepen this lie in our hearts.

Yes, God is sovereign. He is in total control. Satan must ask for and wait to receive permission to attack and hurt people, certainly God's people. We have two clear examples of Satan doing this in the Bible. And both times God says yes! This should be incredibly sobering.

It's safe to assume Satan asked God for permission to tempt Adam and Eve in the garden. And God said yes. Satan asks permission to attack Job. God says yes. Satan asked for "permission to sift" Peter, meaning to tempt and try him (Luke 22:31). God said yes.

Adam and Eve were sinless in the garden when tempted. So was Jesus in the wilderness. God says Job is the best guy on planet earth when he is attacked. Peter was Jesus's number one disciple when he came under fire. Personal holiness, real spiritual growth, intimacy with God is no guarantee that you will be spared the fiercest personalized attacks from Satan himself. In fact, closeness to the Lord might increase the likelihood of receiving a personalized attack. Please be aware.

Matthew 4:1 teaches that the Holy Spirit led Jesus into the wilderness so that he could be tested by Satan himself. God wants his people to be tried, assessed, purified, and thus proven true. It is good but it is not easy or fun. Please be sober minded. Don't be shocked when hardship comes in our lives.

We have been so blessed in the West in the twenty-first century that sometimes when a little pain and suffering comes, we lose our minds. How can this happen to me? I'm one of God's people! Exactly. Join the

---

11. Knox, *Writings*, 308, quoted in Comer, *Live*, 281.

club. Welcome to life on planet earth. Don't be so surprised. What did you expect? Planet earth is a spiritual battle ground between God and Satan for the souls of men!

Derek Kidner teaches that this is the "consistent practice of God."[12] If you are one of God's people, prepare to be attacked. Be wise. Be humble. Be on your guard.

SATAN'S WAYS

Satan has preferred ways and means by which he likes to work. They are very effective. Satan has been given much power in this world. He was delegated authority from God, but it is real, effective power, nonetheless.

In Matt 4:8–9 Satan offers to give Jesus all the kingdoms of the world. Jesus doesn't correct him. It seems he really had that power. Ephesians 2:2 calls Satan "the prince of the power of the air." This is even after the resurrection of Christ. The victory is won, but the battle still rages. And we are right in the middle of it.

In Job 1:13–19 Job experiences four attacks simultaneously from different directions. Some even seem to come directly from heaven itself. There's a common refrain after each attack. One servant survives each massacre to bring Job the tragic news. The lone survivor comes to Job, tells the evil tale, and ends with the statement, "I alone have escaped to tell you."

Put yourself in Job's shoes for a minute. You are an adult who has three different businesses, three separate revenue streams. You also have seven sons and three daughters. All seems well with the world.

Then one day disaster strikes in tsunami-like fashion. Seemingly out of nowhere—quick, powerful, overwhelming, deadly, destructive—death and destruction come. Four lone servants come to tell you that all three of your money-making operations have been utterly, instantly wiped out. But that's just the beginning. It's small in comparison to what comes next.

All your kids love one another. What a great family! They were having a party together. They were in the prime of life. A tornado came and struck the house, and they all died.

Try to imagine the compound impact of all four pieces of news reaching you at almost the exact same moment—three separate businesses destroyed, and all of your children killed. Another repeated reframe

---

12. Kidner, *Wisdom*, 59.

in this passage is "While he was still speaking" (Job 1:16–18). It almost seems as if one malevolent force was behind all these attacks.

If in one day all your businesses, all your kids, and all your employees save four were killed, how might you feel? And more so, how would you interpret these events? Don't just tell yourself what you think the "right" answer may be. Be honest with yourself about what you would be tempted to think and feel in that moment.

Remember the Sinclair Ferguson quote from the previous chapter. How we feel about God is vitally important for our life and faith. How would you feel about God if you were Job that day? Even if you knew all the right theology how would you feel about your sovereign God?

At minimum most of us viscerally would be tempted to think, feel, believe some version of "God must hate me! Why is he doing this to me?! How could he allow so much hard stuff all at once?"

You may have been raised in a pastor's home with the strongest, most well-informed faith imaginable. Yet it's likely thoughts such as "wasn't God strong enough to stop this or wise enough to not do this or good enough to help me" would rage in your mind and heart when you got hurt, even if you did not fully identify the thoughts clearly in the moment. The temptation to doubt God would be palpable. It would seem so normal in such circumstances.

Satan is an expert. He is still going after God's people in similar fashion today. I have a friend who is incredibly smart and hard working. His parents divorced at an early age. His dad would often promise to come visit him as a child and then not show up. The subtle lie crept in, "My earthly father and my heavenly Father won't come through for me when I need them most."

This man is a theologian who knows God and his word. But when life gets hard, and he must wait, he is often tempted to believe the worst. He graduated from college and seminary with great grades. But as he applied for further schooling, he was sure he wouldn't get in. He did.

Later when he was trying to publish a book, he was hard on himself thinking "It'll never happen." It did. Later as he looked for a job, he was filled with doubt, "I probably won't find anything." Satan did a deep work on this man's soul when he was young and impressionable. He hurt him in a way to make him doubt the goodness of God. He is growing but this is still a battle for him today.

Remember, the more "emotional value" a lie has in your life, the more plausible it will feel and thus the stronger the temptation is to believe it and sin. When we experience hardship in life we are often tempted to think and/or say, "That's not fair," which implies, "God isn't fair. I'm getting a raw deal. I'm a victim. I deserve better!" This victim's mentality can be deadly and contagious. Whole segments of our society have been caught in it in the last decade.

One young man once said to me, "I'm not mad at anyone, I'm just mad at the circumstances." Drill down under that thought process and see where it takes you. If there's no human responsible for the hardship in your life currently, if it's just "circumstances," who's in charge of those? Who are you angry at? This can be so subtle. There's truth that circumstances can make us mad, but we need to trace the logic all the way to the deepest roots. Satan roots his lies in enough truth to be plausible.

I know another woman who was abused by her stepdad as a child. When something like that happens, it is obviously right to say that she was a victim of terrible evil and sin. She has come to Christ and grown since then. I know this is an extremely sensitive and tender topic, and I do not want to treat it lightly. Unfortunately, this type of abuse is increasingly common. Let me be as clear as possible. When a parent, someone older, stronger, and in power, abuses a child it is wicked and evil. It is never the child's fault. It is the adult's sin. It is right and true to say that the child experiencing abuse is a victim. That is not wrong to say. It is not blame shifting.

But Satan does not fight fair or play nice. The abuse may end at some point. The child matures into an adult. Maybe the child becomes a Christian and through counseling can make much progress past the damage done from the childhood abuse. Yet Satan does not let go so easily. He will still use that genuine experience of victimhood in childhood to misinterpret other events later in adulthood.

For the specific woman I know, when life gets hard for her today even though her abuse happened decades ago, she can very easily revert to a mindset that says, "I'm a victim. It's not my fault. I did not do anything wrong. This is just unfair." This woman has made some terrible decisions in relationships and finances that have cost her dearly. Her bad decisions as an adult have brought a lot of pain into her life and into others' lives. Sometimes she will take responsibility for her bad decisions. Other times in the heat of the moment she is quick to blame shift, even if she blames the universe. "I don't know how this happened to me. I don't deserve this!" (At some level, when you blame the universe, you're blaming God.) The lie says to her, "You're always just a victim. It's never your fault. There was nothing you could have done to prevent these financial and relational hardship you've experienced late in life. God's not providing for you."

Do you see how insidious Satan is? He doesn't fight fairly. He doesn't play nicely. He will go to any lengths necessary to drive a wedge between you and God. He will do all he can to drive a wedge between you and the truth, you and reality! The better we can understand how he is doing this, the better we will be prepared to fight. We must work and think to make ourselves prepared for the battle we are already in!

Some of you reading at this point may say, "But I don't think any of this applies to me. I've never suffered any abuse or severe trauma." Don't be deceived. Satan can use the smallest hardship or suffering to insinuate his lies. He doesn't need massive trauma to do severe damage.

SATAN'S WEAPONS

Job passed the first test. God and Job won. Satan lost. Job preserved his integrity and continued to trust and worship God. He maintained his faith in God. He proclaimed his trust in God even when life hurt him (Job 1:20–22).

But Satan is a persevering spirit. He doesn't give up so easily. Much of Job 2 reads like a repeat of chapter 1. Satan goes back to God to ask permission to attack Job again. Now Satan strikes Job personally and physically (Job 2:7).

It's likely that Job makes his way out to the ancient trash heap of the city where trash was burned.[13] This is where people with leprosy went. He's an outcast now because of his pain and the skin disease, which, in ancient times, was often seen as a sign of God's displeasure. His life has been brought low. All businesses were ruined. All kids, dead. His physical body, falling apart and in immense pain. It can't get much worse. And yet . . .

Have you ever wondered why Satan spared Job's wife? I've often thought my wife dying might be the most painful thing for me to suffer, and yet Job's wife is spared. Satan spared her to use her. His target was Job, and Satan is an expert in the game. Matthew Poole says the "devil spared his wife with cruel intent to be the instrument of his temptations."[14]

---

13. MacArthur, *Study Bible*, 699.
14. Poole, *Commentary on the Holy Bible*, 1:925.

LIES ROOTED IN REALITY

In Job 2:9 she makes her first appearance in the story. She goes to Job in his misery and airs her thoughts. She gives unsolicited advice. "Curse God and die." Now don't get too mad at her. Put yourself in her shoes. Yesterday all your babies died. She seems to have held her peace on the first day of tragedy. Today, her husband suffers excruciatingly. She breaks. Who can blame her? We may have said the same thing in a rash moment. But there's more going on here. Matthew Henry comments on this strategy:

> Satan . . . provoked . . . the best friend. . . . Skillfully is the temptation managed with all the subtlety of the old serpent, who is here playing the same game against Job that he played against our first parents. . . . She was spared . . . for this purpose, to be a troubler and tempter to him. . . . "Is this a God to be still loved, and blessed, and served?" . . . Be your own deliverer by being your own executioner; end your troubles by ending your life.[15]

In Job 2:3 God praises Job in the heavenly court saying, "He still holds fast his integrity." In v. 5 Satan replies, "He will curse Thee." All this language happens in the heavenly throne room, far out of the hearing of Job and his wife. We are granted behind the curtain access.

Notice in Job 2:9 exactly what Mrs. Job said: "Do you still hold fast your integrity? Curse God and die!" It sounds as though she has been listening to the heavenly court. She obviously hasn't. But it has influenced her. Somehow Satan has influenced her thinking and even her words. She mimics the language of heaven and of Satan.

We are not 100 percent clear on how Satan can do this but it is clear that he can. It does not mean that she was possessed. Satan can and does influence the thoughts of people, even true followers of God. John Gil, the reformed Baptist commentator, commenting on the servant in Job 1, states, "So Satan ordered it. . . . Satan put it into his mind to say."

Acts 5:3 is a New Testament example of this reality. Peter says to Ananias, "Why has Satan filled your heart to lie to the Holy Spirit?" We also know that in Matt 16, right after Jesus has declared Peter to be a genuine believer, Satan influences Peter to try and steer Jesus away from the cross.

We may not understand exactly all the nuances of this reality. But we must be aware that we are subject to it so that we can be prepared to fight. We must daily be ready to push back against Satan's subtle influences.

---

15. Henry, *Commentary*, 466, 543.

Job's wife believed a lie in that moment that said, "God is not worthy to be worshiped, and my husband's life isn't worth living anymore." Whether she knew it or not, Satan used her to try to influence Job to believe the same thing. This is important. When we start to believe Satan's lies then we become pawns in his war against others. We must be on guard. Satan is certainly playing the same game against us.

If you walk down the street and meet a random homeless person and the person becomes angry and yells at you, it may bother you in the moment but not much afterwards. If someone you don't know at all screams at you, "You are an idiot!" it will likely have little to no effect other than being strange. But if your best friend or spouse says the same thing it may devastate you. Satan is so clever in how he pursues us.

I mentioned in the last chapter a woman whose mother died. Another part of her story is that her father abandoned her family when she was young. Her interpretation was that God must not like her much and didn't want her to be happy. She later commented that her father's leaving almost derailed her life: "My dad's leaving almost defined"[16] my life. That is Satan's goal. Bring painful events into your life, get you to interpret them in ways that make you believe horrible things about God, then define your whole life by that "reality."

APPLICATION

It would be good for you to put the book down right now and spend time praying and thinking. Maybe grab your Bible and turn to Job 1–2. Prayerfully ask yourself what hard things in your past and current life is Satan using to try and make you believe false things about God. How is he trying to define your life by these events and beliefs? Before, you put the book down let me give a few more thoughts and examples that may help you discern Satan's pursuit of you.

The goal of this chapter is to get to the deepest roots of sin in our lives. Why do certain lies about God seem to hold so much emotional weight and value in my life and in yours? The lies that sink me are different from the lies that sink you based on our different personalities, upbringing, and life experiences.

That Satan personalize his lies to each one of us is a crucial point. It doesn't have to be severely traumatic to be deeply significant. Satan

---

16. Key, *Stay Married*, 287–88.

can use trivial things to do a deep work. You don't have to have an abusive father to doubt God loves you. Satan's lies can find roots in our lives from smaller things, such as spending lots of time bored and lonely. Deep down you feel it's unfair that you are alone so much. It doesn't seem right to be so bored when so many other people on social media look so constantly happy. God owes you fun, doesn't he? You've been a good person. This tiny thought and tiny lie can feel very real and powerful and lead to a night or even a lifetime of gluttony, drunkenness, lust, or worse.

The Puritan Jeremiah Burroughs writes, "You worship God more by [contentment] than when you come to hear a sermon, or spend half an hour in worship, or an hour in prayer, or when you come to receive a sacrament. These are acts of God's worship, but they are only external acts, to hear and pray and receive sacraments. But [contentment] is the soul's worship, to subject itself thus to God. . . . In active obedience we worship God by doing what pleases God, but by passive obedience we do as well worship God by being pleased with what God does."[17]

There are two main ways to discern the main lie in your life you believe. One is to start with your most obvious, frequent, besetting sin. It may be something as small as complaining. Trace it to its root. Find the "logic" behind the sin. If you dig deep enough, you'll find the fundamental lie.

The other way is to think about the most significant negative events in your life. What was it that Satan was trying to influence you to believe in that moment? If you dig deep enough, it will likely lead you to the same lie your besetting sin does. There is a relationship between the two events, the past trauma and the current sin struggle. One helpful exercise is to try and write down the top ten to fifteen negative things you have experienced in your life. Then try to discern what lie Satan may have been trying to insinuate in you in that moment. Do you notice any themes repeated?

If we can learn to better understand how, when, and why Satan lies to us personally through circumstances it will be easier to catch lies and fight them at the root level rather than at the fruit level where it's often too late. This is the goal of the book. Dig deep. Discern the lie. Kill the lie. Free ourselves with God's truth from Satan's lies and our ongoing patterns of sin.

---

17. Burroughs, *Christian Contentment*, 120.

My wife and I got to know a man who had grown up in a good church and seemingly great family. He worked for a ministry for a while. The lie he believed most was something like this: "God's not going to control the world in a way that will be best for me." So, he subconsciously reasoned, "I have to control as much of the world as I can in such a way to protect and provide for myself." Hearing his story would help you understand.

He had a dad that was passive. On top of that he had a mom that spent most of her time volunteering at the church for ministry events, thus neglecting the family to some degree. The son did not feel he got the emotional help he often wanted or needed when he was dealing with a problem at school.

Now, this man has certainly grown and become aware of this lie and the sinful desire to control life. But in the heat of the moment, he does what we are all tempted to do. He reverts to his old ways. He's lived that way for twenty plus years. Old habits die hard. Especially habits of the heart. Under pressure we revert to muscle memory.

He was in a hard season of life. He was in college but not getting the respect he wanted and thought he deserved from friends in his fraternity nor from ministry leaders he worked with. His response was to try and speak up louder and louder to tell people how spiritual he was and how he ought to have more leadership roles. His strategy had the opposite effect. It led people to tune him out and ignore him.

He and I talked about 1 Peter 5:6 and how he should let God exalt him and not seek to exalt himself. He agreed but then started a verbal battle with himself in front of me. "I know I should just be quiet and trust God to do what is best for me in the perfect timing. But these guys are putting others in leadership roles that don't know what they are doing. I have ideas that could really help! They ought to listen to me more . . ." On and on it went. It was so sad and so hard. The lie was so deep and powerful, it was as if he couldn't stop himself from saying and doing things that were pushing his friends further away.

Why am I telling this story? It is so easy for us to know lots of biblical truth in our minds and believe it and be willing to die for it. But in the basement of our hearts, in our emotions and affections, Satan's lies often still loom large and powerful. When hardship comes and we revert to our old ways in the moment of temptation, how will we respond? Will biblical truth and convictions guide our behavior? Or will Satan's subtle lies steer us away from God in the moment of pain?

The emotional value of the lie in this man's life was so strong. He didn't really start trying to fight it until it was almost too late. Once he's in the middle of the sinful fruit it produces, and he's triggered emotionally and flooding mentally, the battle is essentially over. We must learn to fight sin at root level early in the day.

Hebrews 3:13 says that Christians can "be hardened by the deceitfulness of sin." Satan's lies seem so true and plausible that they control us. John Piper is immensely helpful on this point:

> Would you agree that the only reason you sin is because you believe, at that moment, the lie of the sin, that things will go better this way? Or at least the charge of the moment will be worth the misery of the consequences. . . . [Satan comes in] and gives boosters to my sin. . . . Sin is rooted in me. . . . Sin says to you, for example, the only way you'll have any future is if you get an abortion. That's one of them. . . . Sin only has power through promises. . . . The only reason any one of you sins is because you believe those promises. . . . Here's the deep problem: sometimes these lies get into you when you were small . . . and the deception of sins began to layer themselves over, creating a pocket of almost impenetrable conviction that this must be so. I really can't be happy unless, and let sin fill in the blank. . . . And the layers are so thick that if someone . . . says that's wrong, . . . there's no touching it, it is so deep and so powerfully rooted beneath all the layers of deception that sin has used. That's why verse 12 [Heb 4:12] is in this book—to give you an encouragement . . . that the promises of God are powerful. . . . [The word of God] starts assessing with promises.[18]

Where do Satan's lies have the most emotional value and power in your life? Wrestle with this question today. The better we understand how Satan has lied to us in the past and continues to do so in the present, the quicker we can catch the lie at the deepest root and kill it before it starts to blossom into full flower. Once sin has exploded in our lives it becomes much harder to kill.

So, how do we fight this? Just like Job, we constantly speak the truth to others and ourselves. And we meditate on the truth. We use the truth to focus us back on the goodness of God and worship him in spirit and truth!

After all Job's kids died, he said, "The LORD gave and the LORD has taken away. Blessed be the name of the LORD" (Job 1:21). He means, "I

---

18. Piper, "Word of God," 26:03—32:38.

don't deserve anything good from God. He can give whatever he wants. He can take away whatever he wants. Either way, he is always still worthy of my worship, trust, and praise." Job 1:21 would be a great verse to all memorize, study, meditate on, journal over, and when temptation comes, preach to ourselves! There's power to kill sin in this truth.

Years ago, I had some severe back pain that made it almost impossible to even sleep at times. It was maddening. I was so frustrated. I meditated over and over on the truth that what Satan means for evil, God means for good. God uses Satan's schemes for my good and his glory. God is always faithful, always trustworthy, and always working to bless his people even when it seems the opposite is true. I used verses like Gen 50:20, Rom 8:28, and the whole story of the life of Joseph in Genesis to keep myself in a place of trust and not anger. But it was a daily and sometimes hourly battle. This fight is not for the faint of heart.

CONCLUSION

A righteous sufferer ultimately defeats Satan. This is true in two ways. It is true in a small and incomplete way when you and I suffer well. Every time you and I suffer in big or small ways and are tempted to believe falsehoods about God, the battle is raging. In those moments, we must take those tempting thoughts captive to Christ and believe the truth about God even when it doesn't seem true.

Job did this in chapters 1 and 2. He praised God. He accepted hardship from God. He would not curse God. He continued to praise and trust God even when his wife tempted him away, even when he suffered.

If you had an abusive dad and that fact has led you to believe God hates you, I understand that temptation. But you must hold on to eternal truths that say God is love. If you just struggle with being bored and lonely on Friday nights, it may not seem that you are believing lies about God, but dig deep and see what is the logic behind your restless frustration that pushes you to eat and drink too much. When we suffer well with faith in God's goodness he is honored. Even if that's only the small suffering of self-denial to honor and please him.

In the truest and fullest sense Satan was defeated finally by the one and only fully innocent sufferer. The righteous Lord Jesus Christ was the most complete defeater of Satan. His holy life, death, and resurrection ends Satan's work in a full and final way.

Jesus came to earth to live and die in the place of sinners like you and me. He was not just cast out of the city onto the ash heap. He was cast out of the good presence of his own Father into the true ash heap of eternity—Gehenna, the lake of fire. Christ suffered hell on the cross for my sins of not trusting God's goodness. He was burned for all the sins of all the people who would ever doubt his Father yet ultimately hope in him.

He was faithful in our place. He died trusting the Father. He suffered while meditating, praying, and quoting truth from God's word. He persevered to the end and never once doubted nor accused his Father. He suffered sinlessly for all his people! Hallelujah, what a Savior.

"Father, into Thy hands I commit my spirit" (Luke 23:24). He died in faith. He died believing. He died trusting. He died resting. He died passionately committed to the belief that God is good and trustworthy, even if God is killing you. He died under the wrath of the Father for all his people.

Rest in his finished work. Rest in his life and death and resurrection as the ultimate sign of God's goodness, love, power, and wisdom for you. Then go and sin no more!

When tempted to doubt and sin, preach the cross to yourself. When tempted to fear or worry, meditate on his record of faithfulness for you. Remember his historic goodness so that you can be free from the lies Satan spews.

Chapter 4

Layers of Lies

Matthew 3:16—4:11

Let's review what we've covered so far. Godliness consists of trusting, obeying, and enjoying God. Satan came into the garden lying, tempting, and implying falsehoods about God. He essentially said, "Don't trust or obey or enjoy God. You can't really trust him. Obedience isn't worth it, and you won't be able to enjoy the best things in life if you submit to him."

Satan is crafty and thus roots his lies in reality. He brings thoughts to our minds that seem absolutely true and plausible. We must learn to discern his lies from the truth. We must take every thought captive to Christ (2 Cor 10:5). William Hendriksen, the Reformed commentator, teaches, "For . . . believers, there is, first, the tempting voice or inner whispering of Satan."[1]

Why is this "inner whispering of Satan" so important to understand? If we do not understand this root of sin, we will often be fighting sin at the level of the fruit rather than digging down deep to the root. We may alleviate symptoms of sin, but we won't make much progress in genuine sanctification and maturity. We must seek to understand the deepest roots of our sin.

The deepest root of sin is unbelief, not trusting the goodness of God for us. Romans 14:23 and Heb 11:6 both make this point clear. Trusting God's goodness is the theme of this chapter. Trusting God's goodness would have kept Adam and Eve from sin. Once we doubt God's goodness sin has begun to grow.

---

1. Hendriksen, *Matthew*, 223.

The second deepest root of sin is pride. This pride thinks, "If God won't provide for me then I will provide for myself. I must!"

St. Augustine said, "All sin is a lie. For no sin is committed save by that desire or will by which we desire that it be well with us, and shrink from it being ill with us. That, therefore, is a lie which we do in order that it may be well with us, but which makes us more miserable than we were. . . . The source of man's happiness lies only in God, whom he abandons when he sins."[2] He goes on to speak of pride as a root of sin. "And what is the origin of our evil will but pride? . . . By aspiring to be self-sufficing, he fell away from Him who truly suffices him. . . . Secret ruin precedes open ruin."[3] This chapter will explore this root of pride as well. This root of pride grows out of doubting God's goodness.

Some readers may be unfamiliar with the idea of Satan lying to us. We can miss how directly it applies to our daily life. I led a Bible study once where we started by talking about where we doubted God's goodness in our lives. One of my good friends honestly thought and responded, "I really don't think I doubt God's goodness in any area of my life." But at the end of the Bible study, he confessed that he had really been struggling with pornography recently. He wasn't making the connection, and I often don't either. But it's not hard to see if we slow down and think. He didn't think God was good enough to provide him the sexual pleasure he wanted in marriage, so he pridefully sought that pleasure through porn. He doubted God's goodness and provision. This led to pride in providing for himself in sinful ways.

Sinful temptation to watch porn didn't just start with a lustful thought gone wrong. It's much deeper than that. He may not say these thoughts out loud, but I guarantee they were present in his subconscious. I know this because I've often seen similar thought patterns in my own mind. It's easy to start to think and feel like "I'm a good guy. I'm trying to be a great husband and dad and church member and boss. When do I get to have a little fun for myself. I deserve some kind of reward! I need a little pleasure! I want to escape for just a little while! God's not giving me good stuff in life right now so I must grab it on my own."

If such a thought pattern comes at the wrong time we are in trouble. If we are traveling a lot, alone on the road, and our wife has been sick a lot, it can seem like we are being set up. Sin still lives in us as believers.

---

2. Augustine, *City of God*, 445.
3. Augustine., *City of God*, 460–61.

Satan seeks to provide opportune times for our sinful desire to free itself and grab with gusto. If we aren't careful and on our guards, we are goners.

Imagine if you grew up poor and always worried about money. As an adult you have a fantastic job, plenty of savings, and no debt. But lies about God not providing for you financially and materially still sit deep in your heart. You are often tempted to overwork.

Maybe you recently had a few large, unexpected medical bills come through. And insurance refused to help at all. You start to worry and fear. Then your boss texts you with a special opportunity for extra pay. The boss is offering double pay for anyone who works on Sundays. You don't really need the extra money. You know it's best for you to rest and worship on Sundays. But you are tempted to say yes to the extra shifts. Why is that? Is there a lie in your heart about God's lack of provision for you and your need to go the extra mile to provide for yourself? Satan is an expert in putting us into circumstances to expose us where we are weak.

We must learn to catch these lies, thoughts, and temptations at the deepest levels. The sooner we catch the wrong thought patterns, the easier they are to kill. When we let them grow and fester, they gather strength as a snowball rolling downhill can turn into an avalanche. Let's look at the greatest example of fighting sin—the Lord Jesus himself.

WHAT DID GOD SAY?

Matthew 3 and 4 present us with the beginning of Jesus's public ministry. First, John the Baptist baptizes him. God the Father and God the Spirit show up in an enormously powerful and obvious way to bless and affirm the Son. He is anointed for his calling. He is empowered for the ministry ahead.

The Father speaks audibly from heaven: "This is My beloved Son, in whom I am well-pleased" (Matt 3:17). Life can't get much better than this at the experiential level! But immediately after this Christ is led, by the Holy Spirit, into the desert to be tested by the Father and tempted by Satan. Why does this happen to him?

Ever since God put Adam in the garden with the one prohibition, life has been a test for humanity. Christ came as the second Adam to be our example, our helper, and much more. His temptation enables him to best be able to help us in our temptation as Heb 2:18 and other passages teach.

Jesus's test in ways mirrors Adam's. Genesis 2 portrays God as the perfect Father. He saw Adam lacked a wife, so he made him one. He wanted Adam to have all he needed for life, godliness, and joy. He spoke to Adam. He walked with Adam. He provided lavishly for Adam.

To be experts at fighting sin we must be experts in meditating on Scripture. Further, we must gather up truth as logs for a fire of devotion. We must constantly be throwing new fuel into the furnace of our love for God. Preach the gospel to yourself. Preach your own history to yourself. Remind yourself of all the practical ways God has already provided generously for you. Meditate on passages such as Gen 2, Matt 3, and Heb 2 to help bring deliverance from temptation. Read these three passages and think about how God provides for his people lavishly, how he speaks to us lovingly, and how he walks with us in our hardship.

Part of our sinfulness is that we are so quick to forget the goodness of God. This is not a memory problem. Rather it is intentional mental laziness, which is actually a heart problem. We don't love the truth enough and thus don't remember it nor believe it deeply enough. Deuteronomy records the words of God to the nation of Israel as they prepared to head into the promised land. Deuteronomy 6:10–12 says, "When the LORD your God brings you into the land . . . to give you, great and splendid cities which you did not build, and houses full of all good things which you did not fill, and hewn cisterns which you did not dig, vineyards and olive trees which you did not plant, and you shall eat and be satisfied, then watch yourself, lest you forget the LORD who brought you from the land of Egypt, out of the house of slavery." How can this be?!

God is so good he chooses to save wicked people. He raises them from the dead spiritually. He sets them free from Satan and the slavery of sin. He blesses their socks off, not just with spiritual blessings but with tangible gifts they can see, touch, hold, taste, and feel! And what do God's people often do in response? Praise him? Sometimes. Other times, they totally forget him!

We can get drunk on the goodness of God in such a way that we are enamored with his gifts, and we miss the Giver himself. Our hearts are prone to this type of forgetfulness. Our hearts are "prone to wander."[4] We must fight hard to remember God's good words and deeds to us and for us daily.

---

4. Robinson, "Come, Thou Fount," 2.

WHAT DID SATAN SAY?

Satan came into the garden as we have seen with falsehoods. His first set of lies were subtle implications about God. Remember Tim Keller said that all sin starts with the character assassination of God. This is where all temptation starts. "God is not good, he is not wise, he is not powerful, he is not trustworthy," whispers Satan into our subconscious.

But Satan's lies don't stop there. Imagine if a soldier in war wanted to destroy the communication between the enemy's commanding general at headquarters with their frontline troops. The most effective way to do this would be to attack both sides of the communication apparatus. If the soldier destroys the commanding general's radio but not the frontline radios that will do some damage. But if the commanding general's radio is repaired, communication is restored.

But if the saboteur can destroy the radio of the commanding general as well as the radio of the frontline fighters the destruction will be more effective. If one radio is repaired, it won't matter. The other person will still be unable to communicate. The situation will be much more frustrating, confusing, and hard to repair.

In a similar fashion Satan is so crafty. He not only attacks God in his campaign of lies. He attacks God's people. Even if we start to believe truth about God, we may believe so much falsehood about ourselves that the truth about God hardly seems to matter. I have known people who've said, "I believe God is real and loves people. I believe God is a personal God who has personal relationships with people. I just don't believe God can have a personal relationship with me." This person obviously is believing lies about God but more than that they are believing lies about themselves. Satan is happy to let you have your doctrinal purity and theological accuracy if it stays in the abstract. What he cares most about is your functional, concrete, experiential beliefs about God, yourself, and reality.

If Satan can have you at a place where you would pass the theological exam to serve in the most rigorous Presbyterian pastorate in the world and yet not feel any of the reality of the truth you claim to know and believe, he is OK with that. He is winning. Because when pressure and temptation come, we will revert to what we functionally rest on in the basement of our heart and soul.

Think again of Satan's lies in the garden. Not only did he imply that God was evil, trying to keep Adam and Eve down. He also implied that

Adam and Eve were lacking. He insinuated there was something good they needed to have, ought to have, deserved to have, and yet lacked. It was God's fault. But it was also their weakness. There was special knowledge to be had! It was made for them! Yet they lacked it. Satan is wily. He is devious. He often does not state his lies directly. They are hinted at, which can make them even more insidious because they go down so smoothly and start their evil influence before we even realize what is happening. We are just having a rational conversation with ourselves and the next thing you know we are believing outright lies about ourselves and about God.

Look at Matt 4 and the subtle implications made to Christ in these temptations after forty days of fasting. In v. 3 Satan says, "If you are the Son of God, command that these stones become bread." Simple enough and yet there is more below the surface, much more.

It's as if Satan sneers, "Are you kidding me? God is your good Father?! Look at you! You're starving. God is supposed to feed his children right. He owns cattle on a thousand hills. He's not providing for you. He's certainly not providing in a sufficient way. You can't trust him. You shouldn't have to wait for his timing. Are you really his Son? Does he really love you? I'm not sure you're his Son. You don't look like it to me. But maybe you are. If so, prove it. Use your power. What good is having power if you're not allowed to use it? You're about to die from hunger. Do whatever it takes and get something to eat. Who cares if your dad says the fast isn't over yet? Why does he get to be in charge anyway!?"

There may have even been a subtle implication from Satan saying, "I'll be a better father to you than God. I'll provide for you. I'll show you how to provide for yourself." In so many ways, it's like what he implied to Adam and Eve in the garden. And yet Jesus suffers alone, in hunger and in the wilderness.

R. T. France says, "The devil is trying to drive a wedge between the newly declared Son and his Father."[5] And Satan is trying to do that to every child of God. He is incredibly skilled at it. He has thousands of years of practice.

He implies some lack or deficiency in us and some lack or deficiency in God. If either sticks as plausible in our minds for a second or two, Satan is well on his way to ruining relational intimacy between God and us.

---

5. France, *Matthew*, 127.

Our relationship is supposed to be about trusting, obeying, and enjoying. Satan brings doubt, rebellion, and bitterness.

The first temptation to sin is for humanity to abuse grace. We are tempted to use our privileges as God's children to rebel and do whatever we want. Forget the rules, break a few, go for the gusto. Get whatever you want however you see fit to get it, no matter the cost, damn the consequences. That's the logic of sin. This is Satan's logic. D. A. Carson says, "Sonship . . . surely means Jesus has the power and right to satisfy his own needs."[6] If the first main lie Satan ever told was "God's not good," the second main lie he tells is "humans can and should do whatever they want, when and how they want." The first lie sows seeds of doubt in our heart. The second lie leads to pride.

The Geneva Bible study notes on Luke 4:3 say, "Christ [was] being tempted by Satan, first to distrust in God, and lastly to a vain confidence in himself." These two dual lies work together so well. They have plagued humanity since Gen 3.

It's not wrong to eat food or to want friends. It's not wrong for the Messiah to want to be known as the Messiah, to be crowned King, and to have the glory, fame, and fortune that goes with it. But timing and how things are secured are so important in our obedience and our fight against sin.

Satan's temptations to Christ continue with similar logic. "Are you sure you're the Messiah, the Son of David?! You look like a homeless loser. You're all alone. You have no fame, no fortune, no followers, not even any friends to speak of. Look, if you jump from the temple, God will give angels to save you and then you'll be famous. Then you'll have a crowd. Then people will know who you are. Then you'll feel valued. God said at the baptism he was pleased. Well, make him prove it!"

Matthew Henry is helpful again when he says, "The more plausible a temptation is, and the greater appearance there is of good in it, the more dangerous it is."[7] So many of Satan's temptations make logical sense. So many of his lies appeal not to evil and wicked motives but to good motives at the deepest levels. It's right to want wisdom. It's good to want food. It's pure to love beauty. It's honorable to desire friends and companions.

But Satan's ways always involve a sinful shortcut. He cuts out God to get to his gifts. He offers up a sinful path to a righteous goal, making the

---

6. Carson, *Matthew*, 112.
7. Henry, *Commentary*, 13.

right path even more unclear and confusing for us. Notice Satan's second temptation to Jesus in Matt 4 is rooted in the Bible. In v. 6 Satan tempts Jesus to sin, partially by quoting a Bible verse to him. Satan is an expert in taking something mostly good and twisting it into something fully evil in the moment. Please don't allow the inner rationalizations sin makes to lead you down a deadly path. When and how and where we go about satisfying good desires is often how they can lead us into full blown sin and rebellion. Not trusting God leads to sinful actions. Inward unbelief in God's goodness eventually leads to outward self-centered deeds.

WHAT WILL WE SAY?

In Matt 4 Satan tempts Jesus in at least three separate ways. But some of his temptations were multifaceted, appealing to different desires at the same time. He tempts him with food, friends, followers, fame, and fortune. He tempts him with pleasure, power, and prestige. He appeals to his appetites in so many ways. Yet Jesus stands strong against them all. How?

Each time Christ responds in the same way. "It is written." There is an acronym I learned in high school: KISS, meaning, "Keep it simple, stupid." When life seems to be overwhelming and confusing, go back to the basics. When you don't know what to do, do what you know. When you're not clear on all that would be best to do in the moment, boil it back down to the fundamentals of life you are clear on.

Satan comes with his wiles and deception. He is crafty. Consider this: Twice Satan says in Matt 4, as a lead into his temptation, "If You are the Son of God." That could have fallen on Christ in two different ways. It could have landed in a sense to create doubt. "If you really are God's Son (though you really don't look it because you seem so weak and frail and fragile right now) then prove it by making some bread." Sometimes true Christians struggle with such thoughts. We feel so sinful we wonder how God could ever genuinely love us. We doubt if we've truly been saved and adopted into God's family.

Or the temptation could have landed on Christ in a different sense to create pride. "Since you really are God's Son, you're equal with your Father, right? You have all the rights, powers, and privileges he has. You don't have to wait for him and his timing. Do whatever the heck you want. If you're hungry go ahead and break the fast early and make yourself bread. Use your power to serve yourself, your way, right away." Christians struggle with similar thought patterns about being an adopted child of God. "You're forgiven for all your sin, past, present, and future? Well then, if that's so, go ahead and celebrate a little. Sin with impunity. It's already forgiven. You can have your cake and eat it too, in this life and in the next!"

And the reality is sometimes we can vacillate between pride and doubt at the same moment. Temptation can seem so overwhelming and confusing in the moment. Left to our own devices, it is debilitating. But Christ is our great model of how to defeat Satan. Run back to the word. Tether your life and thought patterns and thus feelings, desires, and actions to God's clear word.

Satan has been tempting Jesus to sin by implying God wasn't a good Father who wasn't providing for Christ well enough. He also implied that Jesus lacked good, important, and even necessary things like food. So, Jesus should use his power and privilege to break God's law and provide for himself in his own way and time. Each time a temptation came at Christ he went back to God's word.

Notice he did not quote verses that talked about how great he was as the Messiah. All the verses he quoted in Matt 4 point back to the greatness and sufficiency of the Father and his words. The foundation of practical, daily holiness is belief in God's goodness for his people. Doubting this great truth always eventually leads to sin.

We must fight temptation as Christ did, by meditating on the word. We must learn to see temptation starting at the deepest level possible. We must be quick to catch it and kill it before it grows.

APPLICATION

I started looking at pornography in the fifth grade. I continued to look at it regularly for five years. I think I was a believer at that point in my life. I grew up in a great family, in a good church, and went to a Christian school for a little while.

I could not have articulated any of this back then. But as I've gone back and tried to discern and understand myself, the sinful thought patterns I believed as a child became clear. Satan and sin pursued me with four lies that made this addiction possible in my young life.

First, God is not going to give you the best pleasures in life. God is not good. He is not trustworthy. He is not worthy of your worship and allegiance.

Second, there are pleasures in life I must have if I really want to be happy. I feel like I can't live without them. These pleasures are worth almost any sacrifice to attain. These pleasures felt like life to me.

Third, I will have to sin to obtain these pleasures, but so be it. It's not that bad. It's worth the risk. It's worth the sin. It's worth offending God. Lots of people do it. Don't beat yourself up about it.

By God's grace he really began freeing me from this sin and these lies in high school. But to some degree those lies became highly personal for me and got baked into my mental and emotional DNA at some level. My thought patterns are often infected with these lies to this day. Their shadows linger long.

John Mark Comer wisely writes, "If you let that lie into your body, into your neurobiology, you let that lie give shape to your behavior. . . . Ideas have power only when we believe them. . . . They have zero effect on us unless we begin to trust them as an accurate map to reality. At that point, they are animated by a strange kind of energy and authority and begin to release life or death into our bodies."[8] So today, I'm forty-seven years old and have been in full-time ministry for over half my life. Yet, those lies can still exercise a powerful influence in my mind when I allow them to, when my guard is down, when I am tired and alone.

Someone developed the acronym HALT to describe when we tend to be more prone to temptation. When we are hungry, angry, lonely, and tired, beware! Think about the last time you clearly rebelled. Were any of those four realities at play? Jesus was hungry, alone, and likely tired when Satan came after him. For me, in present-day life, it may no longer be a temptation to pornography. The same pattern of lies is behind something much more subtle like gluttony.

Maybe I have had a long hard week. Friday night comes, and the rest of my family has plans. I am alone, bored, and frustrated. My wife and daughter may have made cookies before they left. One cookie would be reasonable. Two might be OK. Three would be a splurge for me. But I honestly feel entitled to the whole plate—all twelve, especially while they are warm. Is this healthy? No. Is it wise? No. Is it best? No. Will I regret it? Of course. I don't care. Down they go!

This may seem like such a small thing. But it is sin, nonetheless. God says we should seek to honor him even in how we eat (1 Cor 10:31). He cares about the physical health of our bodies (1 Cor 6:15–20). Overeating

---

8. Comer, *Live*, 35, 46.

is a sin. It is wrong to let our physical appetites rule our decision making (Phil 3:19). God promises to provide all the joy we need (Ps 16:11). When I feel the need to stuff my face full of warm chocolate cookies to find joy in life, I've abandoned my faith in a good, providing Father for a moment and started to trust my own wisdom more than his.

You don't have to be in a desert, starving and alone, to fall into sin. You can just be lonely, tired, and bored on Friday night. Comer is so helpful on this topic:

> If you seize autonomy from God and do your own thing with me, you'll be better off.
>
> This is the lie underneath all other lies. . . . Thought patterns are the primary vehicle of demonic attack upon our souls. . . . Have you ever had a thought (or a feeling or desire) that seemed to have a will to it? . . . If we give in to . . . the thoughts at war with life and peace, they become strongholds in our minds and hold us in captivity. . . . You fight the devil's lies by simply choosing to not think about them. . . . You replace the devil's lies with God's truth. You cut new neural pathways that eventually take root in the neurobiology of your body itself. You become what you give your mind to. . . . (Directed attention) [sic] can literally rewire your brain. When an unwanted thought comes into your conscious awareness, all you must do is think about something else. . . . The key is not just to think about Scripture, but to think Scripture.[9]

Neurobiology and the Bible agree. Romans 12:2 instructs us to "be transformed by the renewing of your mind." Hebrews 4:12 tells us that God's word can pierce and "judge the thoughts and intentions of our heart." Christian maturity comes in part from having God's word in our mind like a sieve or a matrix. As competing thoughts, feelings, attitudes, or desires come into our hearts and minds we must be quick to take them captive. We must hold them up to the standard of God's word. If thoughts do not fit with God's word, we must jettison them and drill down deep on holding onto and believing and trusting, at a deeper level, God's word to us.

Evagrius, a fourth century monk said, "Whenever a thought is not firmly set in one's thinking, so that one can answer the evil one, sin is easily and swiftly handled."[10] This is true spiritual warfare in its most basic

---

9. Comer, *Live*, 63, 86–88.
10. Evagrius, *Talking Back*, 49–50, quoted in Comer, *Live*, 87.

form. Satan will seek in diverse ways to plant thoughts in our minds that aren't true. As soon as we are aware of their presence, we must mentally fight to make sure they gain no ground, find no landing spot, and do not sprout roots in our hearts and minds.

Notice in Jesus's battle with Satan in the wilderness he did not quote random verses—for example, "In the beginning . . ." He recalled specific verses that addressed the specific temptations Satan had brought to his mind. Satan had a temptation about bread. Well, Jesus had a verse about bread. We must learn to do the same.

One great practice is to use our morning time alone with God in Scripture as a time to daily prepare for the fight ahead. Know yourself. Know your besetting sins. Know the patterns of temptation you may face in any given day as best you can. Then mine the Bible that morning for promises and commands that can help you combat the coming lies. Ask for the Holy Spirit's help as you search for truth that will help you with the coming fight for the day.

When God told Adam not to eat of the one tree in Gen 2, God was preparing for the fight that was coming. God knew Satan would come to tempt Adam. God was giving Adam his word to prepare him for the fight. But Adam did not cling to the word as he should have. We should view our daily time with the Lord as preparation for the fight that will inevitably come.

In high school, lustful thoughts and actions seemed to be a near constant temptation. I often felt overwhelmed. My dad told me to memorize Rom 6 and then quote it anytime I was tempted to lust. It was incredibly helpful. Still today, thirty years later, often when tempting thoughts enter my mind, I will quickly start saying to myself, "What shall we say then? Shall we go on sinning that grace may increase? By no means! We died to sin; how can we live in it any longer? Or don't you know that all of us who were baptized in Christ Jesus were baptized into his death? We were therefore buried with him through baptism into death in order that . . ." That's the first three or four verses of Rom 6 in the New International Version, which I memorized when I was sixteen years old. It's still with me.

God's word is like a sword with which we can pierce and kill temptation. It gives strength to our soul in the fight. It removes power from whatever you may be facing. Oftentimes temptations will seem impossible to resist unless you are strong in the word.

One of the things we are attempting to do in this book is to better understand the roots of our sin so that we can kill them. As I look at two sins in my life that I have struggled with often over the years, lust and gluttony, they both have very similar roots. I am looking for a sense of pleasure, joy, and fulfillment in life. I am tempted to break God's law to have immediate gratification in his gifts rather than in him alone. So, I memorized Ps 16:11. It says, in part, "In Thy presence is fulness of joy; In Thy right hand there are pleasures forever." What I genuinely want is joy and pleasure. These are not terrible things. They are wonderful things God invented for us as gifts. Food and sex can be two legitimate ways to experience them in this life. But we must only seek joy in food and sex in the ways, times, and places God intends. Otherwise, there will always be a bitter aftertaste that backfires on us.

So, often now when I'm bored and tempted to eat like a horse to find joy, I will catch myself. I'll talk to myself. "Food won't satisfy you. It may give short-term pleasure. But the best pleasure, the best joy, the cleanest joy, the purest pleasure is in God himself. I need to seek him, trust him, obey him, and wait on him. In his presence is fulness of joy." I may have to persevere in such prayer and meditation for thirty or more minutes before temptation subsides. But this is the fight of faith.

Some of you reading at this point may think, "I don't struggle with anything scandalous like porn. I don't really think demons are trying to influence my thinking." Maybe not. But remember so many of our sins can look white collared and domesticated, like gluttony, small lies, lack of boldness in evangelism, anger in traffic, holding a grudge against someone, and much more. Remember what C. S. Lewis said. Satan doesn't care if he makes you a magician or a materialist. You can be a heroin addict or approval junkie who's addicted to pleasing people and winning their praise. Both can ruin your soul eventually. All Satan wants to do is ruin your childlike trust in your heavenly Father. And Satan is an expert in this fight.

Some may ask, "Is something as small as overeating really that big of a deal?!" Adam and Eve threw all of humanity into ruin and chaos by eating the forbidden fruit. The Lord Jesus began to win back planet earth through discipline in eating. Small sins lead to big sins. Small steps of obedience lead to larger patterns of obedience. And the deepest root of our obedience, in the short run and the long run, is believing God is good. Faith in God's goodness towards us is the foundation on which a life of holiness is built. Discipline and self-control will not be able to stand overall unless there is a constant undercurrent of meditation on God's love and kindness for his people. God's character is the foundation of our fight for faithfulness.

CONCLUSION

There's a fourth lie I have been tempted to believe that I did not mention earlier. It says, "Once I have sinned there's so much shame and guilt, I can never tell anyone. I can't really trust God's grace enough to cover me in the act of confessing sin." I still struggle with this lie today. Do you?

Satan seeks to set us up to sin. He seeks to put us in circumstances that will confound and overwhelm us. Satan did the same thing to Christ. He sought to get him alone, hungry, and tired. He did his best to stack the deck against Christ, but it wasn't enough.

This is where Matt 4 takes on a much greater significance for us. Christ is an example to us of how to fight sin. He is our sinless model. But he is so much more. The main way to read Matt 4 is like a scared Israelite soldier hiding in the ditch as Goliath mocks your God and your people. And then the true Son of David marches forth in absolute confidence, all alone. The wilderness temptations were the official beginning of Christ's conquest of planet earth and humanity. He came to set his people free. He came to defeat the prince of the power of the air.

You see the real temptation in this whole sequence for Jesus was much more subtle and only implied more than clearly stated. Jesus came to earth to take earth back from Satan. In the third temptation Satan essentially said, "Just bow down, worship me, and I'll give you everything you ever wanted or needed! Skip the cross and still get the crown. Take a short cut. Worship me and I'll give you the entire world back."

Jesus came to win the world back from Satan. He wanted to accomplish this. This was a good and right desire Christ had in his humanity. But Satan presented a sinful way to accomplish the good goal. Jesus was wise to say no. Jesus is our faithful example of how to resist any and every temptation at every turn. But he is so much more than that. When we fail to follow our example, he is our Savior, our substitute, and advocate before the Father's throne.

Jesus was so good, so wise, so pure, so patient that he loved his Father fully and faithfully no matter what. He always trusted his Father in all ways. He was more than willing to embrace the scorn, shame, and suffering of the cross to honor his Father and to save sinful people like me and you. He was faithful in life and faithful in death. He was the perfect substitute who always perfectly obeyed in all the ways we so often sin and fail and falter. He took the wrath we so fully deserve.

Hebrews 2:14–15 and 17 say, "Since then the children share in flesh and blood, He Himself likewise also partook of the same, that through death He might render powerless him who had the power of death, that is, the devil, and free those who through fear of death were subjected to slavery all their lives. . . . Therefore, in all things He had to be made like His brothers so that He might become a merciful and faithful high priest in things pertaining to God, to make propitiation for the sins of the people." In times of temptation look to God's word so you can fight against temptation like Jesus did. But even more importantly, in times of temptation and in times of failure, look to the Word incarnate, the God man, the living Lord Jesus, Christ the victor. Look to him to bring you out of sin, out of shame, and out of our failure and condemnation. Romans 8:1 reminds us, "There is therefore now no condemnation for those who are in Christ Jesus."

Jesus is the second Adam. When you trust in Christ, he is your substitute. He represented you on the cross under God's wrath. I had an appointment with God's wrath. The Father sent Christ as my proxy.

Trust in him! He is worthy. Every day I must remember his love and mercy. As we savor the sweetness of his goodness to us in his life, his death, and resurrection, we will be changed, slowly but surely. We will gradually be set free from sin to walk in newness of life.

Chapter 5

Killing Coveting

James 4:1–10

In Gen 2 we witness God creating a world perfect for mankind. He created a good world for people to live in and thrive in. He filled it with good gifts such as food and friends that we might learn to trust him, obey him, and enjoy him and his gifts.

The word for "pleasing" in Hebrew (*chamad*) shows up in Gen 3:6 and in Exod 20:17. In Gen 3:5 Satan lies and implies that God is not good and that the humans are not adequate. He insinuates that they don't really have all that is best for them. Following this temptation the woman looks at the tree and sees that it is "desirable" (*chamad*) to make her wise. Exodus 20:17 says, "You shall not covet" (*chamad*). The root of the word is to desire and to take pleasure in. What can we learn from this pattern?

One of the main goals of this book is to expose the deepest roots of sin. The last chapter focused on the deepest root of all sin, unbelief—specifically, doubting God's goodness. (It also briefly touched on pride as a second root.) This chapter focuses on the next two roots after doubt—namely, pride and coveting. In pride we think we can and must provide for ourselves where God is failing. In coveting we find specific ways to provide for or promote ourselves that fall outside of God's plans and boundaries for us.

God made his world full of good gifts for us to enjoy in proper ways and at proper times. These gifts are pleasing and desirable. Food tastes pleasing. Trees look beautiful and bring a sense of pleasure to look at and enjoy.

But Satan comes in and twists and perverts our desires and pleasures. Ignatius of Loyola said that sin is an "unwillingness to trust that what God wants for me is only my deepest happiness."[1] This fits exactly with Satan's line of logic to Adam and Eve in Gen 3: "You can't trust God. He is not out for your best. He is holding you down. He is keeping the best pleasures, the best gifts, away from you. You ought to be desiring the one thing he's forbidden, for that's the best pleasure to be had!"

Once that lie sinks in, they start to believe God would not take care of them. The next logical conclusion is that if God will not care for me, then someone else must do it. Who can that be? If God won't provide for me, then I must provide for myself, and who cares about the consequences if I must break some of God's tyrannical rules?

The first root of sin is doubt that God will provide. The second is the pride that assumes I can do a better job. The third root of sin is coveting. I begin to look for a gift to satisfy me in an ultimate way that God cannot or will not.

Another way to say the same thing is that sin starts in fear; fearing God won't take care of me. This fear leads to a sense that I must be in control. Then this desire for control starts to look outward for the things I need to secure and/or satisfy myself.

Once we start to feel doubt and pride in our souls that we must and can provide for ourselves, we will look at all things in a different light. It's not wrong to notice a tree looks beautiful. It's not wrong to think that the fruit would taste pleasing. Nor is it wrong to even think the fruit might be desirable because it does provide some special knowledge. The sin of coveting is when we start to think and feel that we must have the forbidden fruit to be happy.

This Hebrew word for desire (*chamad*) is really a neutral word. It can be used in positive or negative ways. It depends on the context for how we interpret it. In the New Testament the Greek word used to translate covet in Exod 20:17 is often translated as lust. The Greek word just insinuates an ardent desire. It doesn't only refer to sex but anything we desire strongly.

It's not wrong to appreciate the good gifts of God. It's not wrong to desire the good gifts of God, such as fruit, bread, wisdom, friends, money, sex, or reputation. But when you say, "I cannot be happy unless I have this certain gift my way, right away," you are in sin. You are coveting.

---

1. Ignatius of Loyola, quoted in Comer, *Live*, 61.

KILLING COVETING

Coveting is a self-centered, corrupt, controlling craving. It is a disordered desperate demand. You desire something, some person or experience, too strongly.

Simon Kistemaker says, "When we discard checks and balances, desires get out of hand and, so to speak, become pregnant. . . . Desire is able to conceive when man's will no longer objects but yields."[2] John Piper is also helpful. "Don't desire anything in a way that would undermine your contentment in God."[3] Thomas Manton, the Puritan author, says, "Lust worketh two ways, by force and fraud. . . . Discontent is plain rebellion."[4] Sin lies to us and then tries to overwhelm us with sinful desire and make us follow its design.

It's not wrong for a man to desire to have sex with his wife. It's right for him to find the experience pleasurable. But if he begins to desire another woman, that is coveting. It is lust and is sinful because he is allowing desire and pleasure to draw him away from God's good design, plans, and boundaries.

It's not wrong for an employee to want encouragement and acknowledgment from their boss when they do an excellent job. But if they desire this praise too much they can begin to covet. They may begin to subtly exaggerate how much they contributed to a certain project to secure a compliment. They have crossed the line by lying to secure approval. A good desire turned into a sinful demand and then led to outward acts of sin.

There are three main rivers of coveting. First John 2:16 sums them up for us. "For all that is in the world, the lust of the flesh and the lust of the eyes and the boastful pride of life, is not from the Father, but is from the world." The lust of the flesh are our appetites for physical things like food, drink, sleep, and sex. Adam and Eve wanted to taste the forbidden fruit. Satan tempted Jesus to make and eat bread while he was supposed to be fasting.

The lust of the eyes has to do with beauty and aesthetic pleasure and possessions. The forbidden fruit looked beautiful. It was attractive. Satan offered Jesus all the riches of the world. This is where greed comes in.

The boastful pride of life is about accolades—being important, noticed, and known. The tree would make them wise. Jesus's leap from the temple would bring instant stardom; it would surely draw a crowd and

---

2. Kistemaker, *Exposition of James*, 270.
3. Piper, *Living in the Light*, 60–61, 79.
4. Manton, *James*, 93, 338.

give an immediate sense of power and significance. Even if no one saw the event, he would experience a sense of reassurance.

On the surface we can sum these temptations up as food, fortune, and fame. But the deep desires underneath have to do with satisfaction, security, and significance. These things in and of themselves are not sinful. In fact, they are good God-given desires. The key is to make sure we always submit these good desires to God's timing and designs and boundaries. When our desires go haywire and become demanding, we are in sin. We are coveting. We are lusting.

We don't all covet the same things. A friend of mine teaches that each of us tends to covet "whatever we think will provide the security, peace, love, and acceptance we lost in the garden of Eden."[5] To overcome sin well we must know what gifts of God tend to capture our hearts affections too much.

It is not sinful for a tempting thought to pass through our minds. These thoughts went through Jesus's mind. When Satan tempted him with bread, Jesus heard what he said. The thought would have passed through his mind that he could make bread and satisfy his hunger. But he did not give into that thought. He did not entertain it. He did not acquiesce. Manton says, "Suggestion can do nothing without lust."[6]

Imagine if I was struggling financially. Someone heard my problem and suggested I murder my wife and collect the insurance money to pay bills. I would hear what they said. I might think, "Yes, I need money. Yes, I guess that may technically work to get the money I need." But that thought would find no landing ground in my heart and mind for a myriad of reasons. I love my wife. I have no desire to kill her. I don't want money that bad. I have a desire for money, but not a sinful desire. In such a scenario I could honestly say I didn't sin. Tempting suggestions were made to me but they found no place in my heart. They appealed to normal, good, and right desires. It's not bad to want money to pay your bills. It would be sinful if I wanted the money so much, I considered murder to get it.

Now, consider if a friend suggested I cheat on my taxes to save money. Imagine he's an accountant and tells me he can cook my books for me so I will never be caught. Unfortunately, that suggestion might pique my interest. (Don't worry, I don't think I'd really do it!) But I could

---

5. Brock, *Errors Parents Make*, 192.
6. Manton, *James*, 93.

see my sinful heart for just a second, considering and rationalizing. "Our government is so wasteful. They spend money on terrible things I disagree with. What's a few thousands of dollars from me compared to the trillions they have?" At this point, though I've not outwardly sinned, I have sinned inwardly. I'm coveting. I'm greedy. I'm lusting after money. I'm willing to consider a sinful strategy to address my desire for money. Because I'm considering breaking laws of a God-ordained government, which I shouldn't do according to Rom 13:1–5.

Desire in and of itself is good and right and God given. But when we allow desires to break God's boundaries, we are already sinning (even if outward actions or words do not occur) by lusting and coveting. We desire something in that moment of sin more than we desire to please and obey God and that is sin.

If I decided to get a second, part-time job to make more money and thus pay my bills this may very well be wise. It's a good desire to pay my bills. It's good to find a legitimate, non-sinful strategy to do so. Desire is not bad. Desire is good and God given. But we must be careful to pursue our desires only ever in God-approved ways.

KNOW YOURSELF

As we discuss sin it is easy to fall into the trap of becoming an expert on other people's sins while remaining willfully ignorant of our own. It's easy to think, "I know there are people out there who have affairs and do murder their spouse for money. But I would never even consider such things!" Maybe not and that is a wonderful thing. But what do you struggle with? Do you worry about money incessantly? Do you watch scandalous TV shows that stir sexual lust in your heart? Are you consumed with trying to manage your image in front of your friends? We all have sins we struggle with. A large part of the battle against sin is knowing our sins and temptations so we can fight them before they even start.

As you read this chapter and book it will be helpful if you will prayerfully seek to discern what are the major areas of sin in your life. What are the main, repetitive ways you are tempted most often? Where do you most frequently stumble into sin?

And if you honestly think you don't know the answer to the above questions, ask your spouse, your best friend, or closest family member. They'll have a good idea. Ask them to be honest and don't get mad at what they say. Manton wisely said, "Noonday devils are most dangerous."[7] He is referring to sins in our lives that don't seem scandalous at all. There is a sense of "everyone does it," that seems to make it feel normal and as if it isn't a big deal. Sins that don't look that bad can be the worst. We tend not to take them seriously. We don't grieve over them. We don't fight them. We tolerate them. Slowly but surely, subtly, they grow, they consume. We grow hard, calloused, and compartmentalized.

We must do the arduous work to investigate our own hearts. James 4:1–3 is immensely helpful in this regard. "What is the source of quarrels and conflicts among you?" (Jas 4:1a). Ask yourself this. Where do you tend to get into the most fights and arguments with others? Even if it's not an external hot war of words. Where do you tend to have internal war with others in your own head? You may only give them an icy stare or the cold shoulder. But often in our minds we have an ongoing conversation with ourselves about what we would like to say. "I can't believe she spoke to me that way?! I'd love to give her a piece of my mind! She needs to hear how selfish and stubborn she is! I can't put up with this any longer! And I won't!"

James answers his own question. "Is the source not your pleasures that wage war in your members?" (Jas 4:1b). Pleasure as we have seen is not a bad thing in and of itself. Pleasure becomes sinful when we demand to have it our way right away. If you show up for dinner and you really want the biggest piece of chicken, that is not a sin. If someone else grabs it first and you shrug and think, "No big deal," and move on, that is not sin either. But if you begin to pout or complain or shout or argue or even fight, your pleasure in the chicken has led you to sin.

James walks us through the progression. "You lust and do not have; so you commit murder. And you are envious and cannot obtain; so you fight and quarrel" (Jas 4:2a). James probably doesn't mean here that Christians were killing one another. Although our sinful desires can certainly lead to that if left unchecked.

James probably has Jesus's teaching from Matt 5 in mind. Sinful anger is akin to actual murder. Sinful anger that erupts in sinful words is miniature murder in the heart just getting its start. We kill others with our harsh and hateful words. We fight and argue, driven by our strong desires.

---

7. Manton, *James*, 98.

KILLING COVETING

A further point emerges as well in v. 2. Our coveting rarely happens in a vacuum. Typically, we see something someone else has, whether it's a car, a ring, a watch, a body, a job, or a reputation. Then we begin to envy them. We want what they already have. And often we feel like we deserve it more than they do. The tenth commandment is against coveting. Don't have a demanding desire for what others have and you lack.

This is one reason social media can be so damaging. It is not evil. But it can cater to the worst parts of us. Most people tend to post their best moments. We see pictures and videos of great parties, friendships, and vacations we weren't a part of. There's no problem in admiration. There's a right way to rejoice as friends rejoice. But if you sink into the comparison game and feel that you are losing, it's not only sinful—it can be detrimental to your mental health. It can cause so much anxiety and even depression.

Again, social media in and of itself is neutral. It can be used in great ways to share baby pictures or to share the gospel! But it can also lead us to be deceptive in the face we present to the world. When we become experts in only taking pictures and telling stories that paint us in a beautiful light, we are essentially lying to others and to some degree to ourselves as well! Worse, there is also a tendency to become radically self-centered and self-interested, even self-consumed. What I am thinking, feeling, doing, etc. begins to feel like the center of the universe, and I must make sure as many people are as aware as possible. This mindset will not help our issue with coveting. It will feed the inner lie that whatever I want, I deserve!

Often our desires in themselves are not sinful. What we want is good things. Our problem is that we are not content to wait on God's timing and ways to obtain those things. And herein lies the problem. We should pray and ask God to provide good things for us in his time and his way.

Jesus taught us to pray, "Give us each day our daily bread" (Luke 11:3). We can apply that principle to any legitimate desire. "Give me today a date to homecoming. Give me a raise from my boss today. Give me tonight great sleep." All of these are good desires. The key is to trust God to determine your best portion of all things each day and gladly to submit to his plan.

Godly prayer includes submission, patience, and present contentment. Coveting wants none of those things. It wants my way right away. Sometimes we do pray and still don't get what we want. There are many reasons. James 4:3 tells us a major reason is "because we ask with wrong motives."

There are really two ways to covet. The first way is a bad desire. I want something that is forbidden for me. Adam and Eve desired the forbidden fruit. Adulterers desire someone else's spouse.

The second way to covet is to want a good thing too much. A single person may have a good desire to be married one day. When it turns into desperation and demands, they are in sin.

But underneath all desires, if you trace them down deep enough, are good God-given desires. All our desires can be traced back to three main things: satisfaction, security, and significance. God made us to want these things. When he created humanity, Adam and Eve had these things. They had food, sex, light, beauty, and cool breezes for satisfaction and pleasure. They were in a safe garden where God dwelled with them and would protect them; they were secure. They had a sense of purpose as the keepers of the garden; they were significant in God's created order. But Satan sinfully led them to desire even more. Sin promises to give us more when we already have all that is best for us. Even in this fallen broken world, we must trust that God still rules all things providentially with pristine wisdom so that we have what is best for us now. See Ps 84:11 and Rom 8:28 for more on that fact.

SUBMIT YOURSELF

James 4:4 accuses coveters of being "adulteresses." He means that when Christians covet, we are like a woman who commits adultery against the most perfect husband of all time. Many places in the Bible compare God to a husband and his people to his wife. Ephesians 5 is the most famous. When we choose to sin, we are making the most insane choice of all time, just like Adam and Eve did.

James goes further and says, "Friendship with the world is hostility toward God" (Jas 4:4b). The world here represents the world system still ruled by Satan. It is a system built on coveting. Think about how much of our economy is built on making people covet what others have.

James 4:5 is a hard verse to translate. It can mean God jealously longs for his people, which is true. Or it may mean that our sinful spirit is always jealously desiring things in the world that we don't really need, which is also true. The bottom line is that the Christian is in a war of desire. God has strong desires for us. We still have strong desires for sin. This war will rage to some degree until we see Christ face-to-face. Even the great apostle Paul still seemed to struggle with coveting. See Rom

7:7–25 for his testimony about that. There will be times we feel stuck in a sin pattern or even addicted to something that is ruining our life, whether that be alcohol or porn or human approval. Even then there is hope.

There is a greater grace (Jas 4:6a). It is literally mega grace. It is great grace. But if you stay proud in your sin, you'll never know this greater grace. If you want to know and experience this great sanctifying grace, you must humble yourself. "God is opposed to the proud but gives grace to the humble" (Jas 4:6b). Remember all sin starts with doubt. Doubt leads to pride. Pride leads to coveting. To sever the root, we must attack our pride and our doubt.

My wife and I have friends who used to work for a church. The husband's employment ended in a hard way. My wife ran into his wife and asked where she attended church now. She was honest that she hadn't been in years. She didn't even try the excuse many make by saying she watches online a lot. Her excuse was given they knew so many people at so many churches in town, any church would be awkward for her because of how her husband's employment ended.

My wife told me about it and was shocked. Part of my wife's shock came from the fact that this woman had been so gifted and effective in ministry. It was shocking that she could just walk away from the church altogether while still claiming to be faithful to Christ. I responded that sometimes gifting goes to your head. Sometimes you can be so "spiritual" you start to think you're above the rules. Biblical rules apply to others but not to me, some can think. My wife responded, "I've never experienced her that way. She must be so hurt she's trying to protect herself." Exactly.

Think for a moment about how the pattern we've discussed applies here. My friend was hurt by the church. Almost certainly there was an internal struggle essentially asking, "God, how could you let this happen to me? You didn't fight for me, protect me, help me, or vindicate me!" The doubt that God won't provide creeps in. Pride comes next. "Well, if God's not going to vindicate my reputation, I'll have to protect myself. I can't keep interacting with these people regularly who may not think well of me. I trusted God. I did all the right stuff, and this is the thanks I get!" It's so easy to slip into a deserving, entitled mindset. Coveting comes next. "I must have protection. I must have friends I'm comfortable with always surrounding me. I cannot be put in any situations that are socially hard and awkward!" A good desire becomes a demand and the rationalization to quit church altogether is well on its way. We are experts in disguising and excusing our own sin. We are masters of covering over our pride with fig-leaf excuses. They may seem to work for us. God sees through them all.

This woman wants security and safety relationally. That's not a bad desire at all. It's a great desire, a God-given desire. But when that desire becomes so strong we are willing to make clearly sinful choices to obtain what we want, then we are obviously in sin and need to repent. Hebrews 10:25 commands us not to neglect assembling with Christians. My friend's hurt drove her to think she was above that command.

In one sense fighting sin is not that complicated. It is hard, but it is simple. If I told you to get on the interstate nearest your house and walk for one hundred miles, that is not complicated. Put on shoes and get to it. But it could be incredibly hard. That's a long way. The weather may be terrible. What about food and rest?

James 4:7 makes the Christian fight about as simple as it gets. "Submit therefore to God. Resist the devil and he will flee from you." Whenever a temptation to sin presents itself, don't do it. Obey God. Resist temptation long enough and it will let up.

Why does James bring up Satan at this point? He's not been mentioned at all in the passage yet. Because as we've addressed in each chapter, there is a real spiritual power that is out to hurt us. It's not just an indwelling sin. That would be bad enough. It's not just a sinful world system that we live in. There is also a real spiritual entity with legions of demons out to get us. The battle is real, and we must be prepared.

As we looked at in the last chapter, Christ is our great model. He was tempted in all three ways. Each time he submitted to God and his word. He resisted Satan and eventually Satan left. The same pattern will prove true in our life if you resist Satan's schemes.

HUMBLE YOURSELF

James 4:8 instructs us to do all we can to practically live closely to God relationally. Fervently practice the means of grace. As you do all you can to draw closer to God, he promises to come near to you. This is a staggering promise. "Draw near to God and he will draw near to you" (Jas 4:8a). I can't tell you how many times I've quoted this verse to God in prayer. As I may be struggling with a strong temptation I may stop and start quoting a verse to myself like Ps 16:11. Then I'll pray and say, "God, you told me if I would draw near to you then you would draw near to me. I trust you, Father. I'm fighting to not give into doubt and temptation. I need your grace. I need extra grace! This temptation feels strong. Please draw near, Father. Please protect me from the sin I'm so tempted to do. Please keep your promise and give me the mega grace I need to say no to sin! Don't let me do what I'm already considering doing! Stop me, please!"

God answers prayers like this. If he didn't, I wouldn't be where I am today. I certainly wouldn't be authoring this book.

But what do you do if you do sin? What do you do when you do eventually give into temptation? The same principles apply. Stop sinning as soon as possible. Confess your sin to your heavenly Father. Repent. Turn away from it to him and his grace. Pray for mercy, forgiveness, and cleansing. Pray that he will help you move on and avoid temptation next time. Don't live divided between two spiritual lovers, Christ and your sin. Commit to Christ fully afresh. Pledge by grace to not repeat the same sin out of your love for him and his great mercy.

James 4:9 tells us we ought to feel appropriate grief when we sin against our Savior. If you did commit adultery against a spouse whom you loved dearly you would feel terrible and rightly so! Likewise, when we sin, there is an appropriate guilt and shame we should feel. Guilt and shame are not necessarily bad. What we do with our guilt and shame is important. (There can be false guilt and shame for things that aren't sinful. But when we've sinned, we should feel bad about our sin. But we shouldn't wallow in these bad feelings!) Rather, confess to Christ and believe the goodness of the gospel. Shake off the guilt by grace and move on in freedom and joy like David did after his affair with Bathsheba and murder of Uriah. He did weep. But he also returned to normal life.

Let shame drive you to Christ and never away from him. If your shame doesn't drive you to Christ, it will eventually, inevitably, lead you back to sin. We are all made to experience joy. The best joy is intimacy with Christ as we experience his love and grace. If you don't return to him to know his mercy afresh you will go back to some sinful practice looking for a counterfeit experience of joy.

If we consistently live humbly before the Lord, he "will exalt" us (Jas 4:10). Part of that exaltation or lifting is the progressive victory we will see over sin. It will be slow but sure. It will be two steps forward, one step back. It will often be painful and excruciatingly slow. At times we will seem to make no measurable progress. But over the long haul of perseverance there will be noticeable, real, tangible growth, change, and conformity to Christ!

To humble yourself means to rank yourself under someone. Remember your place. He is God; you are not. He is the Master and Creator. You are the servant and the creature. Constantly put yourself in a place of trust, loyalty, and submission to your King. Manton teaches that our "sense of weakness should not be a discouragement but an advantage. . . . All God's aim is to bring you upon your knees, and to take power out of the hands of his mercy."[8] This is hugely encouraging to me because I often feel so weak when tempted! But God loves to humble and then help sinners like you and me.

In summary, when you have sinned, the first thing to do is repent. Stop whatever sinful thoughts, words, or deeds you find yourself in as quickly as possible. If you haven't sinned yet, do all you can to fight, to resist, to run. Pray and beg God for help, strength, and grace to fight well. Pray that he won't let you be overwhelmed by temptation.

APPLICATION

To fight sin well and consistently we must know ourselves well. We must be clear on our besetting sins. We must be prepared daily for the fight. That's a lot of what the Lord's Prayer is about. Pray, specifically, "Don't lead me into that same temptation again today, Father!" (See Luke 11:4b.) We don't all struggle in the exact same way. This book is meant to help you become an expert on the unique ways you are regularly tempted so you can fight back.

James 1:14 says, "But each one is tempted when he is carried away and enticed by his own lust." John MacArthur offers a helpful insight. "'His own' describes the individual nature of lust—it is different for each person as a result of inherited tendencies, environment, upbringing, and personal choices."[9] Manton agrees. "Every one hath a particular several inclination to this or that sin rooted in his nature."[10]

I have a friend who years ago noticed a pattern in himself and confessed to me. He would go to work, have a grueling day, come home stressed, and proceed to get drunk most nights because there was more stress at home with his wife and kids than there was at work. Part of my advice to him was quite simple. Pull over in a parking lot somewhere on

---

8. Manton, *James*, 350.
9. MacArthur, *Study Bible*, 1927.
10. Manton, *James*, 93, 347.

the way home and pray to God for grace to be holy between getting home and going to sleep. That's three to four hours max. Jesus taught us to pray daily, "Do not lead us into temptation" (Luke 11:4). What if we did that?

What if each morning, as we spent time alone with God in the word and prayer, we saw it as preparation for the battle that we knew would come? Spend the time meditating on promises from God to meet the deep desires of your heart so you won't be pulled into sinful pursuits later in the day. And don't pray these prayers randomly and generically. Rather, make specific plans, goals, and applications based on your best estimates of how sin will attack you that day.

Tim Keller teaches that in this life there will always be a cosmic ground note of disappointment.[11] So don't be surprised when it comes! No matter how good and godly your life is, there will still be pain and longing on planet earth. No matter how blessed and holy you are, you are not home with Jesus yet, so there will be some good desires that aren't fully fulfilled here and now. This is ripe ground for Satan to sow his sinful seeds. Christians should live daily like soldiers going into battle with our spiritual sense alerted and aware. Be on the watch daily against sin, Satan, and self.

Even in Eden, before the fall, Adam and Eve weren't always satisfied! That's how temptation slipped in. We won't be fully satisfied until we see Christ physically. Don't be shocked when temptation comes. Don't be surprised when your soul seems to rumble for sin. Be prepared to fight!

Know yourself and your sin patterns. Then lower yourself. Humble yourself before God and submit to his word, ways, and wisdom. Get as close to him as you can through the word, prayer, worship, meditation, fasting, communion with other saints, and all the spiritual disciplines that help you. Then fight by grace to stay there.

When tempted, one of the best practical things we can do is phone a friend. As soon as tempting thoughts come into your mind, text a friend. Confessing temptation has powerful influence to kill sin before it starts. But we often do not want to ask for help because it is humbling.

I had an experience once where I traveled a lot and there had been a lot of sickness in our home. My wife and I had not been connecting very much romantically. After a long day I was heading home and realized I would be at the house by myself that night. Almost immediately lustful thoughts and desires started to fill my head. My sinful heart started

---

11. Keller, *Counterfeit Gods*, 37.

plotting and planning to try and find something sinful on TV to watch. I knew I had about five seconds before the gravitational pull of my soul would tip in a sinful direction. I knew what I must do but I did not want to do it. I was in a group text with about eight other guys where one of the things we do occasionally is hold one another accountable. I knew I needed to text them and ask for prayer and accountability. But I didn't want to. It's embarrassing! I'm the only minister in the group. I'm supposed to be the spiritual example. But I did. I sent a straightforward text confessing the lust in my mind and asking for prayer and accountability.

It was amazing how instantly about 98 percent of the power of that temptation seemed to vanish. Sin thrives in the dark. Bring it into the light as much and as often and as quickly as you can. Die to your pride and find victory, joy, and relief.

Manton is helpful again. He refers to the Old Testament law about rape. If a man sought to have sex with a woman who was not his wife and she consented, then she was guilty of sin as well. But if she cried for help, then she was not responsible. She had not sinned in the matter (Deut 22:23–27). He teaches that when we are tempted, we should cry out to God in prayer like the virgin being attacked. He points to Paul's example in Rom 7:24: "Wretched man that I am! Who will set me free from this body of death?" He writes, "It's a sign that sin hath not gained your consent, but committed rape upon your soul. . . . A Christian's life ought to be spent in watching lust."[12] We must have a ruthless rejection at the first tempting thought of sin. We must daily be watching for the ways sin and Satan will stalk us.

I had a friend who was on the verge of divorce. She and her husband were invited to a marriage conference. The husband was noncommittal. But the woman wanted to go regardless of whether he went or not. But she was reluctant. She confessed to my wife she would feel embarrassed if her husband didn't come—to be "the only woman there without her husband." It's totally understandable that she wants a sense of significance in having her husband with her and not standing out and looking strange. But even just in telling us the temptation, fear lost power and she ended up coming.

MacArthur teaches that lust "at first may be largely subconscious. . . . The earlier in the process we determine to resist, the greater the

---

12. Manton, *James*, 96–97, 106.

likelihood we will avoid sin. . . . The longer we delay resisting, the more likely the actual sin becomes."[13]

Another important strategy to fight sin is to enjoy as much of God's goodness in his gifts in appropriate times and ways as we can. The more joy we can take in God, the less we will be tempted to seek it elsewhere. So, how can we maximize proper enjoyment in God's good gifts without falling into the slippery slope of coveting more than we have a right to in a certain time and place?

Imagine your grandmother is the best cook in the world, but her cooking process takes a long time. So over Christmas you go to visit, and you look forward to the feast to be served at lunch. Your grandmother knows her reputation for late lunches, so she prepared a wonderful appetizer for you to snack on in the meantime. In fact, she made several.

You and your cousins sit in the den and snack on the amazing appetizers. While you have a snack, grandma cooks. And the smell from the feast wafts in from the kitchen and fills your senses.

The smells are so heavy you can almost taste them. But it's still not ready yet. You must wait. In the meantime, you continue to snack. Some of the appetizers are great. Some are OK. Some have grown cold and stale and honestly aren't that satisfying compared to the feast you know is coming.

You enjoy the appetizers but don't overindulge. Because you know the feast is coming. That's what your heart, soul, mind, and strength are ultimately fixed on.

Life on planet earth is a time to enjoy all God's wonderful appetizing gifts. But always remember they'll never satisfy the depths of your soul. That will come when you see Jesus face to face for the very first time and then it will last forever. His pleasures are in his presence and they last forever (Ps 16:11). I like to say that Christians have the greatest retirement plan of all time: an eternal feast with the King for all eternity!

CONCLUSION

Why is waiting for God's ultimate heavenly feast so hard? Because Satan's lies are so subtly effective in our hearts and minds. We fear that God won't give us the best things in the best timing in the best ways. So out of this doubt and pride we rise to provide for and protect ourselves. We become desperate and enslaved to our desires, which turn into demands.

---

13. MacArthur, *James*, 52.

We want accolades and praise and don't think God will come through. So, we find arrogant ways to proclaim and promote ourselves.

Deep down we don't fully believe the feast is coming. We don't rest in its reality. And we doubt if God really is the best cook in the universe. Maybe Satan has a few forbidden pleasures that would be even better, at least for a moment or two.

We must fight to live with dependent faith and not desperate fear. So much of this boils down to patience. Remember Jesus in the wilderness, tempted with food, fortune, fame, and followers. None of those things were bad. In fact, he got them all very soon after those temptations. He still has them now. He has them fully now in heaven.

We must really believe the promise that God is a perfect Father who always gives us what is best for us. He knows better than we do what we truly need. He promises to give us as much as we need (Luke 11:8).

Faith in the Father leads to obedience, enjoyment, submission, and contentment at all times. Believe the principle that when we humble ourselves to live by faith, not fear, he will exalt us in the perfect place, way, and time, even if that happens to be in the next life! Can we wait for that? In heaven he will give us not only all we need but all we want and much more. He will exceed the farthest reaches of our meager imagination here on earth.

Learn to see the principle of exaltation following humility in all of life. There are two main ways to do that. First, remember God is the Creator of the universe. He created all things and wants us to find ultimate pleasure and joy in him. Therefore, it makes sense he won't allow Satan to have better pleasures to offer than he does.

Manton says, "God hath made man of such a nature that all carnal delights leave impression of sorrow at their departure."[14] So if we pursue sin there may be temporary pleasure in it for a short season, but it will always leave us hollow with a bitter aftertaste and needing more joy (Heb 11:25)—which will lead us to sin in more and often worse ways. Sin never ultimately works for us! It never satisfies your soul. It always backfires. There may be a rush of joy and adrenaline from jumping out of a plane without a parachute. The free fall may be quite exhilarating. But the painful splat at the end will make it all suddenly not worth it!

In fact, sin typically moves you further from your real goal. Whatever the good deep desire in your heart that you are ultimately pursuing

---

14. Manton, *James*, 98.

is can never be fulfilled by sinful means. Coveting in any form is always a black hole of neediness. It will never be enough, no matter how much you get.

"Giving in to the desires of the flesh . . . lead[s] to . . . prolonged suicide by pleasure."[15] It may be death by a thousand cuts. But sin always leads to death eventually. It may be physical death or spiritual death. It might be the death of a friendship or marriage or business opportunity. But sin always leads to death.

Second, the principle of humility leading to exaltation is at the heart of the universe. The clearest example is of the Lord Jesus Christ, who had all the satisfaction, security, and significance in the universe with his Father, reigning in heaven. But he chose to lay it all aside and come to earth to lose it all on the cross where there was no joy, no safety, no peace, and no glory. He fully humbled himself into hell itself. He suffered the loss of all these good things that one day we might share them with him in heaven.

He loved us so much he went into the black hole of God's wrath that we deserve for all our sin and rebellion. All the punishment for all of God's people was dumped on him that day. All the wrath for all our sinful pursuit of pleasure outside of him and his ways was experienced by Christ that day. He satisfied the wrath of the Father that we might be free from the enslaving nature of sin. Why are we so often desperate to return to that slavery!? We are like "a dog that returns to its vomit" (Prov 26:11).

But the Lord Jesus Christ has become our great living substitute and advocate. He was tempted repeatedly, as we are, but always said no. Then at the conclusion of a perfect, sinless life he went to the cross. He died an atoning death, a freeing death. He laid down in my grave so he could save me and prepare me for the greatest eternal feast of joy in heaven. He rose again and ascended into heaven to prepare an eternal place for me (John 14:2–3).

Live for the coming feast. When we have faith that Christ will one day meet and satisfy all our true needs and desires in the deepest and fullest ways, fighting sin becomes easier. It does not become easy, but it is easier.

Live by faith in the risen Savior. Live by faith in the coming feast. Live by faith in the God who loves you enough to purchase the eternal feast for you at the cost of his own blood.

---

15. Comer, *Live*, 123.

Chapter 6

Sin After the Sin

Genesis 3:6–21

We've been looking at the roots of sin. Sin starts with doubting God. We also doubt that we have everything in life we really need. This leads to pride. If God won't provide for me or protect me then I'll provide for myself. This in turn leads to coveting. We look out on the world full of God's good gifts and begin to have a demanding attitude. "To truly have pleasure, I must have this thing. To really feel safe, I must have more money. I must have more experiences like these, or I can never feel good about myself."

John Piper defined Adam's sinful thinking about God in this way: "I don't trust you anymore to provide the best life. I think I know better than you what the best life is. I reject your love. I reject your wisdom. I reject you as my all-wise, all-providing Father. I vote for myself as the sovereign in this relationship. I will do it my way."[1]

In Gen 3:6 Adam and Eve both ate the forbidden fruit. You may think this is where the book should end because sin is born, and thus, we've discovered the roots of sin. But unfortunately, there is more. Sin continues to breed and manifest itself in new ways.

Once sin is in our hearts, it is not content to stop. It grows. It layers over itself, developing a web of hardness over our sinful hearts. Persevering in sin brings truly deadly consequences. Although we are all born into the world with a spiritually dead heart, there is a sense in which that dead heart can become even more hardened and calloused in its sinful

---

1. Piper, *Providence*, 503.

SIN AFTER THE SIN

ways and patterns. The sooner someone repents the better. But sin will always try to prolong and delay that process from ever starting. Once repentance has started, sin and Satan will do all they can to hamstring the process along the way.

There are two important things to take note of before we proceed. The first is to discover who sinned first. People like to debate if it was Adam or Eve. The battle of the sexes rages on! It was neither of them. Satan was the first sinner. Satan sinned against God obviously. But he also sinned against both Adam and Eve by tempting them to sin.

Following Satan's temptation Adam sinned against God, but he also sinned against Eve. Adam did not lead well. He did not protect his wife from Satan. He was passive. Men still sin this way daily.

Eve sinned as well in multiple ways. She sinned against God by disobeying, but she also sinned against Adam. She tempted and invited him to join her in the forbidden fruit. She encouraged him and helped him to sin. She wasn't the strong encourager and helper God made her to be and that Adam obviously needed.

Adam and Eve and all humans are victims. We have been sinned against by other people. Now some may be tempted to quit reading right now because you hate it when people play the victim card. (I understand that.) But I beg you'll stick with me and follow the logic. Many in our culture today want to use the victim card as an excuse for their sin. I promise that's not where I am going. Because that's not where the Bible goes.

If anything, I am trying to cut through the excuse of "I'm just a victim" and heighten the legitimate responsibility we should feel for our sin. Just because we were sinned against and thus a victim does not mean that we cannot also be a willing sinner at the same time. Satan sinned against Adam and Eve by tempting them. In that sense they were victims. But they had an independent will that chose to believe the lies and disobey God. They were victims but also villains.

Some reading this may get nervous because now that we are born dead in our sins we do start out as villains before we ever become a victim. And yet, Rom 5:12–18 teaches a concept referred to as federal headship. Adam was the representative of humanity. When he sinned, there is a sense in which we were present there with him in his loins and thus sinned with him and are thus held responsible with him as well. (See Heb 7:9–10 for another case of the Bible using similar logic.) So, when Adam was victimized by Satan, in a sense so were we.

On top of that many of us in life experience being victimized before we ever experience being the villain. Imagine a young girl who's overweight in elementary school and is made fun of a lot at school. This can be extremely hard for a young child to understand and process. It feels so mean and unfair. Yes, she was born a sinner and thus a villain. But in her experience and memory she was experiencing terrible victimization before she was ever conscious of making a willful wrong decision.

Some may have experienced worse things growing up. Many may not have such a traumatic background. But for most, we experienced others sinning against us, even if it was a neglectful mother or an absent dad, before we ever consciously sinned against someone else. My point is merely that we are all sinners, and we also are all victims to varying degrees.

Secondly, when Adam and Eve first sinned, how should they immediately have responded? The instant they bit the forbidden fruit, and the sense of shame and guilt came crashing in, what should they have done? Sometimes Christian teachers will say, "Don't give me the Sunday school answer," meaning don't try to give the technically correct answer, but rather tell me what you truly feel. But in this instance, I do want you to think of the Sunday school answer. What should Adam and Eve have done in Gen 3:7 as soon as they realized their sin?

They should have run straight to God and begged for mercy! They should have sought God out and cried, "Forgive us!" Rather than running to God and crying for forgiveness, they ran from God thinking, "We'll fix this." "We got this," was their attitude. That's just more sin after the sin. That's just pride on top of their pride. That's just self-deception on top of the deception Satan had already sold them.

Third, before they sinned, they were naked and unashamed. They had nothing to hide, nothing to fear, nothing to fake, nothing to lie about. After they sinned, that freedom and confidence were gone. Ever since sin entered the world, all of us hide from others, hide from God, and even hide from ourselves. Let's look at all these failing attempts.

HIDING FROM OTHERS

When we sin, we feel shame. We feel disgraced. We don't feel right with God. We don't feel right with others. Nor should we.

There is such thing as misplaced shame or inappropriate shame. If someone accidentally spills their drink and friends start to laugh, they might feel shame for that. But they shouldn't. It was a common human mistake. But when we sin against our Maker, we do well to feel bad about it.

As I've mentioned before, I started looking at pornography in the fifth grade. Fairly quickly lies developed in my mind. I couldn't have told them to you then, but they were there.

One lie was "I can never tell anyone." One of the ways sin ruins us is it makes us more concerned with human relationships than with our walk with God. Adam and Eve should've been most concerned with their personal walk with God immediately after sin, but they weren't. And usually neither are we.

Often, we are much more concerned with what other human beings will see in us, know about us, and think about us. Adam and Eve had been best friends, lovers, and perfect spouses. One minute later they don't trust each other.

Now they are afraid. They feel different. They look different than each other. They are suspicious of how the other might view them. What might the other person think about me? How might they feel about me? How might they treat me? I can't trust anyone. What if they take advantage of me? What if they hurt me? What if they abuse me? What if they lie, manipulate, or deceive? All fair questions considering what had just happened.

Their consciences are aroused. They know they've sinned. They know they've fallen from grace. They now feel shame.

A layperson's definition of shame and guilt is helpful at this point. If guilt is "I feel bad because I did something wrong," shame goes deeper. Shame says, "I feel bad because I am wrong. I am broken. I am worthless. I am hopeless."

Again, there is such a thing as toxic shame. We might call it sinful shame. Shame that we should not feel. If someone was molested or abused by someone much more powerful than themself, they might feel terrible shame about it, understandably so. But there was nothing they could do; no way they could stop the behavior. They were innocent of that sin. It was committed against them. They shouldn't feel shame before God for something they did not willingly do. This would be a toxic shame. It is a strategy of Satan. Don't feel shame for something for which you were not responsible. God's love defines you, not the degradation you experienced.

Adam and Eve certainly felt legitimate shame in the garden. They had willingly sinned. They had knowingly rebelled against a perfect God and Creator. Not only do they feel distant from God, but they also feel distant from each other. This distance from each other seems to dominate their minds at first.

When we have been sinned against, we often feel shame for letting that happen to us. This may be toxic shame we shouldn't feel. When we join in the sin, we feel even more shame for that willing participation. This is legitimate shame. For most of us we have both types of shame operating in our hearts at any given time. It can be almost impossible to delineate them. We simultaneously are victims and villains. We feel hurt, embarrassed, and guilty all at once. We get hurt. When we are hurt, we tend to harden ourselves in a type of self-protection. Our guard comes up. "I'll never be taken advantage of like that again," we think to ourselves. We make a vow of self-protection.

When we become hard people, we usually end up hurting others. We don't have the emotional space and energy and safety and security to reach out and love others. We dare not take that risk. We remain guarded and closed off. We distance ourselves even from those we love with our body language, tone of voice, and facial expressions. Consciously or unconsciously, we push others away. Hurt people become hard people. Hard people hurt people. People that feel hurt by life can become like porcupines. Most people in life have a sort of tough exterior in an attempt to protect themselves from future pain. Part of this is cutting them off from relationships. There is a danger in intimacy. Intimacy involves letting your guard down. You might get taken advantage of.

Sin ruins relationships. It separates us from others. Even those we are closest to get pushed away by sin. When we feel guilty and ashamed we can't stand it. We seek to cover it anyway we can. Adam and Eve reached for fig leaves to make loin cloths and aprons to cover their sense of shame. How do you do it?

James Montgomery Boice says, "The nakedness . . . was psychological as well as physical. . . . The most common covering is good works."[2] Calvin is helpful as well. "The sense of shame, which rises spontaneously, [is] a sure token of guilt. . . . [We] are covered with shame at the first compunctions of conscience; but self-indulgence soon steals in, and induces us to resort to vain trifles, as if it were an easy thing to delude God. . . . All bury the disgrace of their vices under

2. Boice, *Genesis*, 235–36.

flimsy leaves."[3] All people sin. All of us feel shame. All will seek to cover. The question is how we seek to cover. We don't use fig leaves. We often use good works.

We are experts in creating new ways to cover up our sense of shame. The main way we do it is to pile enough good works on top of our sin so we start to look a little better than we really are, even to ourselves. We like to highlight our good works for others to see.

Think about social media. Most people post pictures when they look their best, not their worst. Most make a post to Facebook or wherever to highlight a new accomplishment, not a new failure. Many wait until once a year when their house or family looks nice, clean, and happy to allow the world to see them on Instagram. The reality is we have been playing the same game in real life long before social media was invented.

In our relationships we can take on different "personas" that keep people at bay. We can be the tough guy or the tough girl, always with a straight face or a little bit of a scowl. There can be a feeling of safety and security if others are intimidated by you. They'll keep their distance. They won't pry too much. They'll give you your space and respect. This is one of the cover-up strategies I go to when I want to protect myself from others.

I had a friend in the Marines. He told me that drill sergeants in boot camps are putting on a certain personality when they are yelling at their recruits. They are loud, confident, even mean at times. But they may come inside with other sergeants and let their guard down, take off their hat, lower their voice, and talk about how their throat is sore from all the yelling. In an analogous way, you and I can put on a certain "front" when we want others to leave us alone. It is like wearing a mask.

Others have a fun guy or fun girl persona. They are party animals. They have a "devil-may care" attitude. They can laugh at a funeral. They never cry, except when laughing too hard. They can mock anything and anyone. Life is a joke. Don't take anything too serious. Never let the music and the good times stop. There's perceived safety in the distance of a noisy party.

Others may be saccharine sweet—sappy to the point that they are fake and unreal. Too nice to be true. Always smiling, always happy, always deferring, always giving in to others. They never cross anyone. They

---

3. Calvin, *Genesis*, 157, 159–60.

may claim to be peacemakers. But they are counterfeits. Who can be mad at or hurt or disagree with such a peace faker?

Now, God has given us different personalities. Some people naturally smile more than others. Some are more serious more often than others. There's nothing wrong with being yourself. There is something wrong when you turn a personality trait into a psychological suit of armor to protect yourself. Maybe you try to be the expert who's always teaching and coaching others but never able to humble yourself to truly learn from anyone else. There are many different ways to keep others at bay.

Know yourself. I do tend to have a tougher personality and exterior. But the more I grow in Christ, the gentler and more open I become. That doesn't mean I walk around all day now smiling like a clown. But when I'm in the spirit I do try to be aware of the vibe I'm giving off. I do try to carry myself in a way that puts others at ease and invites them into conversation and doesn't push them away.

But if for some reason I don't feel like opening up to someone, I know how to push people away. If I feel like protecting myself, I can give icy stares. I can use harsh language that's like a brush back pitch that says "Don't cross me. You'll pay if you do."

We all have ways we have developed to survive in this fallen world. They serve us to some degree. Overall they harm us. We want to say to the world, "All is fine here. Nothing to see. Keep calm, carry on." "Never let them see you sweat" becomes a life motto.

I have one friend who tends to "power up" when he meets new people. It is as if his voice gets louder, he sticks his chest out a little further, stands a little taller, and shakes hands a little firmer. It is as though he's trying to let people know, "I'm tough. I'm independent. I'm a man. I'm a stud. Don't mess with me." It's not inviting at all. It's off-putting. But maybe that's what he wants at times.

Paul David Tripp has authored a great book about how people in full-time ministry get into sin. It is very instructive for all of us. If it can happen to a minister, it can happen to us all:

> Pride and confession are enemies.... All members of your community are regularly tempted to think that their sin is something less than sin. We're able to name our anger as zeal.... We are skilled at calling our impatience a desire to move forward. ... We are tempted to call gossip the sharing of prayer concerns. Being power and control hungry gets recast as exercising God-given leadership gifts.... Every leadership community needs

to regularly cry out for help, admitting that sin doesn't always look sinful.... This exchange is not a dramatic event but rather a subtle and often long-term process. Likely no one goes into ministry saying 'I am going to make ministry my identity,' but along the way, something happens.... When you look horizontally for your sense of self[,] ... you are all too attentive to the opinions, responses, reactions and situations around you. You look too intensely at how people are responding to you, and you listen too carefully to what people are saying and how they say it. You notice discussions or plans that included you. You are troubled by the advancement of others and quietly envious of their ministry success.... Your hyperattentiveness crushes your peace of heart, leaving worry, concern, anxiety, and/or fear in its place. It is a vicious cycle, because the more you pay attention, the more you find reason to be concerned, and the more you're concerned, the more you pay attention.... When you look horizontally for what you have already been given vertically, the things you look to will always fail you.[4]

How much of that quote resonates with you? What areas of your life are sinful, yet you have recast them as a gift or just part of your God-given wiring? Are you too worried about what others think about you? Are you looking horizontally for your sense of self? Notice the last line of the quote. For Christians, this is such a sad and stupid game to play because we already have all we need in Christ. We are loved; we are accepted; we are safe; we are secure. We don't have to secure ourselves. We must simply rest in the love we already have.

The bottom line is that we are excellent at hiding our sin from others. But this just exasperates our sin. If you struggle with pride, that is sin. But then if you lie about it, hide it, and cover it up, now it is double sin. Now you're not just proud. You are a proud liar. We must stop the cover up game. It's sinful. And eventually, we find out it never works.

HIDING FROM GOD

The main way we know that our fig-leaf righteousness doesn't work is that when God came walking in the garden, Adam and Eve ran and hid. They didn't feel safe and secure. Their coverings provided no real protection. Their self-made efforts to hide were worthless. Still, they doubled down.

---

4. Tripp, *Lead*, 154–55, 167–69.

They experienced a fear of God that wasn't reverent or worshipful. Their fear was servile and sinful. God comes into the garden and as soon as they hear his sound, they run to hide behind trees. God asks, "Where are you?" (Gen 3:9). He was not a detective trying to solve a case. He was not ill-informed or confused. Rather, he is a wise parent trying to illicit an honest confession from a guilty child.

Imagine you tell your child, "No more cookies tonight." You later come into the kitchen to find the cookie jar open and crumbs around your son's mouth. You ask, "Did you eat another cookie?" You're not trying to solve a mystery. You are trying to encourage your child to be honest and humble. You are inviting them to confess.

Adam arranges the words of his reply in Gen 3:10 to put the word "sound" at the beginning of his reply. This is a way to emphasis a word in a Hebrew sentence. Adam is saying I ran and hid because of your sound: "You were too loud. You surprised me. You scared me."

In our shame and fear we are experts at hiding our guilt. We are masters of covering up. One of our favorite strategies is to blame others, especially the authorities. The rules were too strict or unrealistic. Deep down we often blame God.

Shame leads us to hide from others. Fear leads us to hide from God. At least Adam was honest about that.

Satan told Adam he would be more like God after he ate the fruit. It was a lie. He was less like God. He was more like Satan. Satan told half truths to disguise and confuse reality. Adam is now doing the same thing in his answers to God. He is trying to mask the real reason he sinned. He is still trying to cover his guilt and shame from the one who knows all things. Blame shifting is a dead-end path for Adam, for Eve, for me, and for you.

Often, we will start out like tough people. "I'm fine, there's no problem." But if someone pushes just a little and asks a question that convicts us slightly, we can quickly change tactics. We switch gears easily to the victim strategy. "It's not my fault! I'm just a poor helpless victim. I had no choice. I was deceived." We run, hide, cover, cower, and fear.

In modern day life, if you feel the need to hide from God, what do you do? How do you act when conviction is bearing down? When the Holy Spirit seems near, pressing down the guilt you're trying to ignore, how do you respond?

Many people skip church; some just sleep in. Others quit reading their Bible. Others stay away from godly fellowship—anyone who might ask a prying question. Others may still hang out with the same friends, but they will make sure to keep the conversation shallow. Whatever is brought up, they can quickly bring the talk back to shallow waters of froth and meaninglessness. They refuse to pray. They don't worship, meditate, or journal.

What I have noticed in my own life is that I will stay busy. I will cut silence out of my life if I think the Holy Spirit might be drawing near to convict. I'll have phone calls, plenty of people to talk to, sermons to work on, and the radio is always on if I'm alone in the car.

The sad thing is this betrays such a fundamental lie about God I am believing in that moment. God is good. God is loving, wise, and kind. If he does want to convict me of sin, it is not for the purpose of punishing me! It's because he loves me and wants to free me. He wants to do heart surgery on me. It may hurt, but it will help in the long run. If I believe the truth about God, I'll be quick to slow down, to read his word, to pray, to listen, to hear, to repent! God came in the garden that day to help Adam and Eve, not to hurt them. He came to bless them, not to burden them. They expected wrath but got mercy!

HIDING FROM OURSELVES

Maybe the deepest sin after the sin is the way we deceive ourselves. We become so insecure in our guilt and shame we can't bear to face the truth about ourselves. We are sinners. We are villains. We are not just victims. We are willing accomplices with the devil. We partner with Satan in choosing to disobey. We chose our sin. We used our free moral agency to rebel against God.

In v. 11 God continues his inquiry. He doesn't let Adam off with his technically true reasons that dodge the real issue. In v. 12 Adam confesses. First, he blames God, then the woman, and finally he admits responsibility.

How is it that we lie to ourselves? We minimize our sin. We spin, we make excuses, we blame shift, and we rationalize our role in the entire process. We try our best to explain it all away. Eve does the same thing in v. 13: "The devil made me do it."

If you want to emphasize something in a Hebrew sentence, put it at the beginning. If you want to minimize something, put it at the end. Adam's confession says, "The woman whom Thou gavest to be with me, she gave me from the tree, and I ate" (Gen 3:12). Interpretation: "It's her fault God. It was her idea. She started it. Really, you bear blame too. She was your idea, remember? I didn't ask for her. I didn't make her. So, you and the woman conspired to put me in an impossible spot. But yes, technically I guess I did take the fruit out of her hand and bite it. So I bear a tiny bit of responsibility."

MacArthur says about this passage, "The basic reluctance of sinful people to admit their iniquity is established here."[5] Boice agrees and goes further. "We even cover up in the act of confessing wrongs."[6] C. S. Lewis is so helpful. "We have never told the whole truth. We may confess ugly facts[,] . . . but the tone is false. The very act of confessing—an infinitesimally hypocritical glance—a dash of humor—all this contrives to dissociate the facts from myself."[7] Do you see what he's saying? "Yes, technically I did it, but that wasn't really me. I didn't really mean it. That's not truly who I am."

Matthew Henry says, "The excuses men make to cover . . . their sins[,] . . . like the fig leaves, they make the matter never the better but the worse[;] the shame, thus hidden, becomes the more shameful." We attempt to make things better by lying, hiding, and minimizing. Yet, we make things worse. We add to our sin. God came into the garden that day to forgive Adam and Eve and restore them. They ran from his mercy. They put more sin between them and God. They put hurdles between themselves and the grace God had in store.

Technically they confessed. But it may have been the worst confession of all time. It is the barest minimum repentance of all time after God himself basically had to cox them and lead them there by the hand.

This should encourage us. Don't intentionally slack in your confession and repentance. Hate your sin. Flee it. Grieve, wail, and mourn like James taught. And yet know that God is not an angry tyrant measuring the depths of your repentance to see if you are worthy of grace. That's great news because none of us will ever repent perfectly enough to earn any grace. It doesn't work that way. And he is so kind, gracious, loving, tender, merciful, and quick to forgive, he will pursue us even as we continue to compound our sin in our halfway confessions. Don't turn confession into a good work to earn God's favor. Just humbly and honestly confess your sin to your perfect Father.

5. MacArthur, *Study Bible*, 20.
6. Boice, *Genesis*, 181.
7. Lewis, *Problem of Pain*, 44–45.

APPLICATION

Please spend time being honest with yourself about how you attempt to hide from others, God, and yourself. How do you lie to others, God, and yourself? How are you seeking to cover up your sin on your own? How do you seek to fix yourself apart from God?

Often, we start by underplaying the victim card. "There's nothing here. I am tough. I am strong. I am good, godly, and wise. I've got this. I can manage life. I don't need help.

We put our best foot forward. (It's called the false foot. Eventually the other foot will come forward.) We keep our chin up with a stiff upper lip. We never let them see us sweat. Our guard is up. My defenses are ready. My mask of righteousness, tied tight! I never let my slip show. My suit of armor fits as nicely as I can make it fit.

But God sees through all of that. And wise people will as well when they spend enough time with us. We may believe our own lies for a while. But at times, at home alone, bored, and in silence, the truth will come crashing in.

If someone gets too close and asks questions, guilt and conviction may bubble up. We can quickly swing the pendulum to a new strategy. The tough guy becomes the consummate victim. The party animal or fun girl can quickly melt in a pile of self-pity and tears. "Woe is me. It's not my fault. You must understand the circumstances. I would never have done that on my own. I'm so sorry. I'm trying my best. Can't you be patient with me?! I think I'm getting better, aren't I? Please affirm me! I'm so lonely and hurt. People have taken advantage of me. It's not my fault! You don't understand how hurt I am! How dare you ask me these probing questions when I'm the one really suffering over here! My life is so hard!"

Much of this may be true. But none of it is an excuse for sin. People will sin against us and hurt us. We can't change them. We do have responsibility before God for ourselves. On the judgment day he will ask us how we oversaw our personal responsibility.

If both strategies fail, we don't necessarily give up. We can retreat to the inner recesses of our minds and try to convince ourselves it's not that bad. "It could be worse. Everyone is doing it."

More than once, I would have an argument with one of our children and afterwards my wife would ask if I wanted feedback. The honest answer was no. If anything I wanted a compliment. But I'm just barely wise enough to know that I need to hear truth from my wife even when it's not pretty so I would ask her to give me all her thoughts.

I might start by saying, "I handled that well. I did not yell or cuss." She would press through my first response. She can be like God sometimes.

Then my mask might start to slip a little. "Well, honestly, I'm sick of this. He started an argument, not me. He yelled. He cursed. I took it and did not respond in kind. They didn't respect me. Two of the other kids jumped in and ganged up on me." Just pause and think for a minute about the stupidity of a grown man, a minister, in his forties, complaining that three teenagers had started it. Our sin is desperate to excuse itself and will go places that we rationally never would.

I may shut down and go inward (although I hate it when others do this to me). It's like the last line of defense. I think to myself, "She has no idea. There was a ton I wanted to say and could've said and should've said, but I held back. I was freaking merciful if we're being honest. I'm doing better than she knows or ever gives me credit for!" See, now I've become the victim, at least in my own mind. That's a dangerous place to be, cause it's hard to hear constructive criticism when you think you've been hurt or falsely accused. Your guard can go up in self-protection. And it can stuck there so that you can't hear anything, even from God.

Even if you have been falsely accused, be cautious not to defend yourself too vehemently. I have seen pastors falsely accused of something they did not do. They are hurt, angry, and go on the defense. But they become so enthusiastic about clearing their name, it is as if their mind gets stuck in self-defense mode. Then, if someone later brings criticism to them in another area that is legitimate, they cannot hear it. They've trained themselves to defend themselves against anyone who attacks them. This is a perilous place to be. Trust in Christ to vindicate you, not your own arguments.

Our sin separates us from God, others, and ourselves. And even from reality to some degree. Shame, whether it is legitimate or illegitimate, is one of the strongest forces and feelings on planet earth. It can be so deceptive. Be careful. Shame taken in the wrong direction can ruin your relationship with everything and everyone including yourself and God.

At the end of World War I, there was a lowly German soldier who heard Germany had surrendered and wrote, "The more I tried to achieve clarity on the monstrous event in this hour, the more the shame of indignation and disgrace burned my brow[,] . . . this misery. In the days

SIN AFTER THE SIN

that followed, my own fate became known to me. . . . I resolved to go into politics."[8] Do you know who said that? It was Hitler.

The shame he felt as a soldier in losing a war drove the rest of his life. Fear and insecurity drove him to terrible ideas and places. They can do the same to us if we let them.

We may be quick to proclaim, "But I'm a Christian. I know better!" Listen to Ferguson again: "As long as the law uncovers sin in our lives, we are liable to fall back into the old legal view of ourselves. This is why the psychology of the old life can take much longer to shift than its theology. We understand the gospel, yet there is a continuity in the person who lived under the law's condemnation and knew nothing of God's grace in Christ."[9] We can have pristine theology and still functionally feel condemned in our shame and be motivated by it in sinful ways. The psychology of our old man continues to exert influence!

Richard Lovelace agrees: "The human conscience is very deeply disoriented in its conviction that we must have works and sanctification to recommend ourselves to God. We must carry out a very deliberate replacement of this misunderstanding with the awareness that God simply wants honesty, openness, and a trusting reliance on Christ our Savior."[10] That replacement is what this whole book is about. See where we functionally still live according to Satan's lies. Identify them. Repent of them and replace them at a functional, foundational level with God's freeing truth.

Keller explains, "We must have multiple exposures both to our need for God's grace . . . and to the gospel message. To get God's love and Christ's grace down deep into the motivational principles of our hearts, to the foundational layer of our identities, is a process, and often a slow one."[11] The more we cover up and hide and lie, the deeper we get stuck in our sin and thus the harder it is to come out of it.

Imagine for a moment if Hitler had been converted at some point late in life. Imagine all the evil habits, thought patterns, and belief systems he must have developed over such a wicked life. God can do anything. But practically speaking it would have taken so many years of gospel ministry to begin to truly dismantle all that was fundamentally flawed about that man.

---

8. Hitler, quoted in Manchester, *Last Lion*, 651.
9. Ferguson, *Whole*, 121.
10. Lovelace, *Dynamics*, 114.
11. Keller, *Prodigal Prophet*, 219.

The same is true of us. Our sin patterns run so much deeper into the basement of our hearts than we know. We must do the work by God's grace to see the roots so we can attack sin at the deepest level and thus bring lasting change to our lives.

C. S. Lewis said, "The main work of life is to come out of ourselves, out of the little, dark prison we are all born in." And he also warned of the danger of "coming to love the prison."[12] Why would we love prison? It's all we've ever known. At least it feels safe, cozy, and known.

Kidner sums up the sin after the sin this way: "This shrinking from God remains part of our fallen condition.... [Adam's] retreat into verbal hiding only puts fresh obstacles in the way of mercy."[13] Where do we see mercy in this passage?

CONCLUSION

God came into the garden that day as the LORD God. He is the covenant making and covenant keeping God. He is pursuing his rebellious children so tenderly, so patiently, so gently. He asks questions to illicit a confession. He is seeking to draw them kindly to repentance. He wants to show mercy to them. "The kindness of God leads you to repentance" (Rom 2:4b).

Finally, they do confess though it is so weak and minimal. And yet, he is so merciful he accepts their confession. He had to lead them to the water and make them drink, and yet he shows grace.

God had said they would die that day if they ate the forbidden fruit. Yet they continue to live. But Gen 3:21 tells us that "the LORD God made garments of skin for Adam and his wife, and clothed them." How did he do that?

An innocent animal died that day. That animal was slaughtered for the sins of God's people. Adam and Eve now needed clothes. Their own attempts had failed miserably. God's provision would be perfect and full to protect them not only physically but psychologically as well.

This animal's death is a foreshadowing of the Lord Jesus Christ. He came to earth and went to the cross in our place as a sinless substitute. He took all the sin and all the shame of all his people with him to the cross. He was falsely accused, tortured, abandoned, stripped naked, and

---

12. Lewis, *Problem of Pain*, 143.
13. Kidner, *Genesis*, 70.

crucified publicly. He was forsaken by his Father. Can there be a deeper feeling of shame?

All his protective coverings stripped away. He bore the whole weight of the wrath of God for his peoples' sins. It was a terrible and dark day.

The instinct after sin to run and hide is a right instinct. God's wrath is real and terrible and comes for us all in our sin. The problem is we can never hide from God. We can never really run from him.

Our only hope is to run to him. Salvation is to hide in him. We must hide in the finished work of Christ in our place. We must cover ourselves with the blood of risen Savior by faith.

By grace, be dressed spiritually with his righteous life, lived in our place! This should free us from all shame, all sinful fear, and insecurity. This should empower us to be fully honest with others, with ourselves, and with the Lord always.

We can confess our sins ultimately and honestly. We don't have to spin or minimize or negotiate. God has already settled all our accounts when we trust in Christ.

I don't have to put my best foot forward any longer. I can always put my honest foot forward. Christ put his life forward for me. He lived and died and rose in my place. I am free! Free to confess. Free to own up to my sin. Free to repent. Free to be forgiven. Free from shame. Free to grow and be changed by his grace until I see him face-to-face. Live in the freedom Christ has promised!

Chapter 7

Accused and Acquitted

Zechariah 3

The previous chapter focused on the shame and guilt we feel for our sin and how we respond to those feelings. This chapter will drill down deeper into the same reality. Genesis 3 makes clear how Satan lured humans into sin. It does not make clear how he seeks to condemn people after they've sinned. This chapter will focus on that.

Satan lies to us about God and about ourselves. We have seen that with Adam, Eve, Job, and Jesus. Another way to say the same thing is that Satan makes accusations about God and about us.

We've also said Satan roots his lies and accusations in as much reality as possible. His lies about God have no truth in them yet often appear true based on our surrounding circumstances in the moment. Our experiences can make Satan's lies feel very real and true.

Satan's lies and accusations about us are rooted in truth. Because of this, they are often much harder to fight. We will look at an example in the short book of Zechariah.

God's people in the Old Testament made up the nation of Judah. They had sinned terrible sins. They had worshiped other gods and idols. As a result, God sent the Babylonian Empire to conquer them. Much of the nation had been taken into captivity for roughly seventy years as a consequence for their rebellion.

A group of Jews, numbering about fifty thousand, had returned to the promised land under a leader named Ezra. They began to rebuild God's temple, which had been destroyed. The people started well but did not finish the rebuilding project. They were opposed by enemies who did not want them to succeed. They also struggled with sinful desires and indifference to God's plans and ways that led to a shut down in the building.

God sent two prophets, Haggai and Zechariah, to motivate the people to restart the building project. Zechariah received visions from God to help him do this. The vision we will look at in this chapter will remind us somewhat of what we saw in Job.

It is a courtroom scene in heaven. The Lord is the judge. Satan acts as an overzealous police officer or prosecuting attorney. The people of God are the accused defendants.

This vision may seem strange to us and yet most of us have experienced feelings internally of being spiritually accused. We can often feel "not right" with God. We can feel distant and cold, accused, and guilty, just like Adam and Eve in the garden right after the forbidden fruit. Sometimes the thoughts of our mind are like a courtroom drama.

I have a friend who grew up in a godly home and family. He's in his seventies now and very theologically educated. But he told me that from an incredibly young age there always seemed to be a courtroom scene playing out in his mind where he had to defend himself, his thinking processes, and ways of life, before a judge. I think many people can identify with this.

Romans 2:15 says, "Their conscience bearing witness, and their thoughts alternately accusing or else defending them." It is speaking of non-Christians specifically. But this is true of all of us to a degree. We have a God-given conscience that allows us to discern right and wrong. None of our consciences are perfect. Some tend to over accuse themselves. Others tend to under accuse or over defend themselves. The fact is we are all familiar with the battle in our mind, which can sound like a legal case playing out before a judge. "What I did was not that bad, was it? Yes, it was. I know better. I should never have done that. What's wrong with me? Stop it! It's no big deal. Everyone does it."

One point of this entire book is that often, so called innocent self-talk can have demonic origins. Sometimes Satan seeks to help us defend ourselves when we are guilty. Other times Satan seeks to heap on the condemnation when we have done nothing wrong. At other points, we have sinned and yet Satan seeks to drown us in guilt and blind us to gospel hope. We must be aware of his attacks and influence so we can push back against these lies, deceptions, and accusations.

"Our thought patterns, are the primary vehicle of demonic attack upon our souls. . . . Have you ever had a thought (or a feeling or desire) that seemed to have a will to it? An agenda that was hard to resist?"[1] Sometimes we are tempted merely by our own sinful desires that find opportunities for expression in a sinful world (Jas 1:14–15). Other times Satan or one of his minions is there stoking the flames of our sinful desires, feelings, and thoughts (Jas 4:1–7).

Satan starts out as a great tempter. "Come on, jump in! The water of sin feels fine. It's cool, refreshing, and liberating! You deserve this. You've worked hard. You owe it to yourself. In fact, God owes it to you. And the consequences will be worth it." One practical point to remember when we are tempted this way is that the pleasure of sin will never outlast the pain of consequences.

As soon as we jump into the waters of sin, Satan can flip his strategy and become the accuser and condemner. "How dare you sin against God! You are an apostate. You're not real. You're a fake. You are a liar. Your whole life is hypocrisy." He lures us into the river of sin to play and enjoy and then he tries to drown us in shame and guilt. And he is very skilled at both. Jonathan Edwards says, "The Devil has driven the pendulum far beyond its proper point of rest; and when he has carried it to the utmost length that he can, and it begins by its own weight to swing back, he probably will set it, and drive it with the utmost fury the other way; and so give us no rest; and if possible prevent our settling in a proper medium."[2]

Satan doesn't play fair. He is out to get us and separate us from Father God any which way he can. But Father God won't let us go that easy!

ACCUSED

Zechariah has a vision involving a high priest named Joshua. This is not the same Joshua from Exodus and other earlier books. The job of the high priest was to represent the people of God before God all year but especially on the one momentous day of atonement, Yom Kippur. Leviticus 23:27–28 gives more detail on this day.

This was the one time of the year that one human being could go into the holy of holies where the ark of the covenant was. There were ritual bathings and sacrifices preceding his entrance. Further, there was certain clothing to be worn so that the priest would appear clean and holy

---

1. Comer, *Live*, 86.
2. Jonathan Edwards, quoted in Lovelace, *Dynamics*, 260.

as he approached the Lord. External cleanliness in the Old Testament religion was supposed to be an outward sign of inward purity.

In this vision the high priest stands before God's throne and is wearing clothes covered in human excrement. Not a pretty sight. Now imagine if you were in court accused of a crime you committed. Before the trial you bought a nice suit or dress to try to look like a respectable citizen in court. But on the way to court you were covered in mud by a passing car. You now sit in court looking, smelling, and feeling dirty, even as you feel dirty on the inside with your guilt. External appearance is not going to help your case.

How would you feel at that moment? My guess is you would feel helpless, hopeless, guilty, and condemned before the trial even started. Joshua must've felt that way standing before the Judge of all the earth in the cosmic courtroom of the universe. And to make matters worse, Satan is standing right there at his right hand accusing him of sin. And many of his accusations are true!

If the high priest is condemned before God as the nation's representative, it makes sense all the Jewish nation would be condemned as well. In and of himself, he had no hope. Neither do we.

After the Babylonian captivity, the Jews never fell back into some of their worst sins, like worshipping the false gods of the surrounding pagan nations. There had been some real progress and sanctification. Yet they weren't perfect. Sounds like us, doesn't it?

An Old Testament commentator says, "The place of grosser idolatry had been taken by the more refined idolatry of self-righteousness, selfishness, and conformity to the world[,] . . . which gave Satan a handle for his accusation."[3] We may be genuine believers that have experienced real progressive freedom from our sins of old, especially the external and scandalous ones. But we all still struggle with some of the white-collar, domesticated sins such as sinful anger, lustful thoughts, greed, worry, and cowardice.

Often in the lives of Christians, as we grow in genuine practical holiness, our conscience also becomes more sensitive to these smaller sins of the heart. Because of the ministry I am in, I have seen many fraternity men come to Christ while in college. Before Christ, their attitude often seems to be, "I don't have that many sins. I'm a fairly good guy. Yes, I smoke weed and get drunk and sleep with my girlfriend and look at porn.

---

3. Keil and Delitzsch, *Commentary on the Old Testament*, 254.

But if I could just stop those four things, I think I'd be good." Later they come to Christ. They do experience real growth, freedom, and progress. All four of those sins may be removed. What happens? They start to see much more subtle sin. They see their pride, their selfishness, their racism. This happens for so many Christians.

Sometimes when life is hard and painful it can cause us to examine our spiritual life. This can be a good thing. But for some, our conscience can become overactive. We start to think, "Why are all these terrible things happening to me? What did I do wrong? I'm not sure? Is God angry at me? He must be! I must have done something! I'm not sharing the gospel enough. Yes, that must be it. I need to be bolder! Or I'm not serving my wife enough? OK, I'll wash the dishes more." Again, spiritual examination can be good, right, and healthy sometimes. But if we go into overdrive and have an internal witch hunt, that's not good; we may start to imagine sins that aren't even there. Or we may drag sins from the past back before our minds, sins that have already been repented of and forgiven relationally by God. Sometimes we suffer in life not because of specific sin but just because God in his providence may be trying to do something else in our lives that we aren't aware of yet. That seemed to be the case with Job. Suffering is a normal part of the Christian life (2 Tim 3:12). Don't be surprised when it comes.

Calvin said, "We think that God forgets us when he does not immediately succor [help] us, or when things are in a confused state."[4] Beware in tough times of Satan's subtle influence and accusations. We can often feel condemned when life is painful. Christians can feel condemned, cold, and far from God even if they have Rom 8:1 tattooed down their whole arm in large font.

Think about Job. Satan rooted his lies and accusations against God to Job in the bad circumstances in Job's life. Pain can be a great garden for Satan to grow his deception in our hearts. Remember the harsh words of Job's wife. Essentially she said, "God is not worthy of your worship and your life isn't worth living. Just kill yourself." Job stood strong in chapters 1–2. He went on to struggle from chapters 3–41.

Lovelace says, "Satanic forces attack Christians directly in their own minds with disturbingly accurate accounts of their faults, seeking to discourage those who are most eager and able to work for the kingdom. . . . All vital Christians are to some degree 'demonized' . . . defined . . . to

---

4. Calvin, *Commentaries on the Minor Prophets*, 86.

cover every phenomenon from temptation to possession."[5] Please read that quote again slowly. Many Christians fear anything that may sound like a victim theology, one where you quit taking responsibility for your sin. But the reality is there is a real devil, there are real demons, and we are all influenced by them in various times and ways. We must be aware so that we can fight well to defeat these temptations and roots of sin in our lives that hold so much sway over us.

Ferguson agrees. "The children of God hear the whispers of the Evil One: 'Look, you have sinned. You have broken God's law. You are under condemnation. You are not qualified to be a believer'. . . . He knows he cannot destroy the salvation of God's people; but he is bent, indeed hell-bent—as he was in Eden—on destroying our peace, liberty, and joy in God."[6] One of the reasons so many believers struggle through life without much joy and peace are Satan's condemning thoughts. One reason so many hold back in ministry endeavors is overwhelming guilt and shame. Christians often feel distant from God. It should not be. We can have so much head knowledge and so little heart experience.

We need to learn to see how Satan pursues us in personalized ways. He is crafty to develop thought patterns, lies, and accusations that are molded to make the most damage in our minds based on our personality, our background, our upbringing, and the current events in our lives.

I want to share several stories and examples of people that I've been friends with or ministered to over the years. Names are changed so they cannot be identified. I do this to prime the pump to help you discern how Satan might be personally lying to and/or accusing you.

Ed's father died when Ed was young. His mom remarried a man who was emotionally and verbally abusive. Ed became very passive because he feared triggering his stepdad. Because of this he often hears the thought or feels the accusation "You're not a real man," internally. Often as a grown man if someone compliments him, he doesn't believe them because his stepdad's voice is still so loud and powerful in his mind. Satan has used past circumstances to attack his sense of identity as a man created in God's image.

Ted had an older brother who was a great football player. Ted played as well. A coach compared Ted to his brother often. "Why can't you be more like your brother?!" So, Ted quit. He played other sports. He was

5. Lovelace, *Dynamics*, 139, 143.
6. Ferguson, *Whole*, 133.

good and even played in college, but he was risk adverse. He could dunk a basketball easily in practice or in pickup games. He never even tried in a real game because of fear of failure. In his mind he often hears the thought "You're a failure."

He graduated and got his dream job. He got a tough assignment out of the gate. It went OK but not great. It was not his fault that the venture failed. His bosses moved him to another area, and he thrived. But he is haunted by the lie "I'm a failure." He thinks, "Whatever I do, I fail." Satan will find where we are weak and then find ways to reinforce the same lie repeatedly in various times and ways.

Ellen's parents divorced when she was young. Her dad spent little to no time with her. When it was his weekend for her to visit him, he would pick her up, bring her to his house, put her in front of the TV, and go downstairs to work in the garage. He would leave her alone for hours. She began to think and feel, "You are unlovable. Your own dad doesn't even love you." Now, as an adult if someone wants to spend time with her, she's suspicious. She doesn't really believe them. They must want something. This makes her cold, cautious, and guarded, which can make people reluctant to spend time with her. This can then become a self-fulfilling prophecy. Satan is so crafty and wicked.

Shane's dad was his coach. He has a distinct memory of being in a wrestling match and doing his best to win but still losing. His dad was nearby looking at him yelling, "Do your best!" He thought, "I am but it's not enough." That thought sticks with him today in a condemning way, "My best is never good enough." He has a wonderful job. He is paid well. If his wife complains about finances, it goes deep. He feels like it's never enough. If she gives advice on how to better talk to the kids, he hears, "My best parenting isn't enough." If she asks him to take out the trash, even there he can feel like a failure—like he's trying his best, but it's never enough. Remember, his best wasn't enough to win in the wrestling match. But Satan has taken that one experience and tried to define his whole life with it.

Lynn grew up in a single parent home with a mentally ill, abusive mom. She felt the pressure not only to make her mom happy but also to help take care of practical things such as finances. The lie she began to feel was "I must be perfect." She would think, "It's all up to me. If I don't come through and perform, everything is going to fall apart." She still struggles to live under that pressure when things are busy at home or at work today. This can lead to anxiety and worry when the schedule or finances are tight, although she has plenty of time and money to do all God is calling her to do. Her fear and worry have no rational root, but she is tempted to live the same way she learned to live as a child.

I have met multiple people that struggle with the same lie and had very similar experiences growing up. They struggled a little in school. Sometimes they might ask a question for clarity. A teacher might get mad, and kids might mock, laugh, and snicker. So, they quit asking questions, which further hurt their grades. They learned not to talk when intellectual subjects come. They learned to fade to the background. They feel dumb. One man told me the satanic thought that goes through his mind is "something is wrong me with." He thinks, "My brain is broke, and I'll never get better." This too can become a self-fulfilling prophecy. It can lead people to give up in life and thus feel even more like a failure; and so they do not try their best to excel where they can.

Satan is still active in the world today. How does he lie to you? Please take time to think and pray about how he personally accuses you. Even stop right now and maybe spend time journaling about the negative self-talk in your head that might be demonically influenced.

ACQUITTED

The hardest thing about all of this is Satan's accusations have truth in them. Sometimes we do fail. Sometimes our best isn't enough. Sometimes something is wrong with us, and we can act in unlovable ways.

Joshua, the high priest of God's people, was a sinful man. The nation of Judah was full of sinners as well. I am a sinner and so are you.

Ed, mentioned above, is sometimes passive and not as manly and active as he should be. Ted, my risk adverse friend, sometimes holds back and hedges his bets and does end up failing at tasks. My friend who feels his best isn't good enough sometimes just decides to sleep in, do the bare minimum at work, and head to the bar by himself after a short workday. Not exactly a recipe for success. This can just perpetuate the feeling of not being good enough.

My friends who aren't as smart as others sometimes just give up and don't try. One of them dropped out of college. I could go on with examples, but the point should be clear. We have been saying it from the beginning. Satan roots his lies in enough truth to make them very plausible. He weaponizes weaknesses in our lives to try to define us by our worst qualities or our worst experiences.

We all have things in our lives that set us up for Satan's personalized attacks. They land in our soul and feel so true and real, don't they? What are we supposed to do? How should we rightly respond?

There are at least three wrong things to do that won't help and may make things worse. The first response is often to try to cover our sense of inadequacy with good works. We try to answer the accusation all by ourselves. Look at me! I'm really a great person. I'm really working hard. My best is so good. I really am lovable. Look at all I'm doing.

This may work in the short run, but it won't hold up. It will be exhausting and impossible to manage this fake, performing version of ourselves. We will eventually crash. And even when we don't crash, we will feel like a failure on the inside. We will sense we are a fraud. "If people only knew the real me, they still wouldn't like or trust me. I may have done well this time but just wait for me to screw it up the next time." We are not powerful enough to defeat Satan's attacks with our own efforts.

There's another deadly consequence of always putting your best foot forward and never letting your guard down. Even when people really do genuinely show you love and respect, you can't receive it or really believe it. You will feel and say to yourself, "They don't know the real me. They've never seen me for what I really am. If they knew the real me, they'd have no honor, respect, or love for me at all." Your fig-leaf righteousness externally prevents you from ever really experiencing love and grace from others even when they are extending it to you.

Another favorite strategy is just to stuff it. We hide it, brush over it, minimize it, and pretend it isn't real or there. Some reading this book may be scoffing at many of these ideas. "This all sounds like psychobabble to me. I'm a confident Christian man who reads the King James Version Bible every day! Satan's not talking to me." People like that are usually the most insecure and have bought into the lie so deeply it has become a part of their personality. They don't even know it's there because they can't separate their lie from their actual identity.

Sinclair Ferguson is once again very helpful:

> Repression . . . leads to all manner of psychological disorder. In the Christian life that disorder will penetrate from his psychological to his spiritual condition with disastrous consequences. No doubt there are subtle pressures upon us to appear to be better than we are, but to give way to them by repression is fatal. . . . Satan will want to make as much capital out of our indwelling sin as he can—we have all encountered his accusation, "how can

you be a Christian with such thoughts as these passing through your mind?" . . . But only as we face up to them and see them in their full ugliness will we recognize that crucifixion must be their fate. . . . Bring your sin into the light of God's presence. The last thing we naturally do must be the first thing we do spiritually.

It's so easy in church communities to stuff our sins and the lies we believe and try to convince ourselves and others that we are better than we really are. It never works. It always fails. We must be ruthlessly honest with ourselves, others, and most importantly with God in prayer.

The third way people approach these accusations is to run away from community so that they can just wallow in guilt and self-pity. That's a terrible approach and won't work either. Alone with lies, lies will grow stronger and more powerful. We will be condemned with feelings of shame and totally ineffective in life. This is a way to just give into the lie and let it win. "I really am just a failure after all. No one expects much of me, so why should I even try anyway."

So, what should we do? If you read all of Zech 3 you will notice that Joshua never speaks. Not once. He is silent. He does not speak up in his own defense. Is that because of shame? Maybe. It may be wisdom.

Most likely Joshua doesn't speak because he really doesn't have a chance. Satan accuses in the first verse and in the second verse God speaks up. The LORD runs to his defense and acts as judge and defender. God speaks up before Joshua even has a chance to or a need to! This reminds me of Luke 15 when the prodigal son had a speech of repentance memorized to tell his dad. But when he got home, the father ran to meet him and cut him off! The loving father did not even want to hear his whole speech. He welcomed him back before the son could finish.

In Zech 3:2 God rebukes Satan and tells him that he has chosen the people of Jerusalem for himself. He plucked them out of the fiery trial of captivity in Babylon for himself, not so Satan could harass them.

In v. 4 God's actions rebuke Satan. God commands that the sinful deeds and spoiled garments be stripped from the priest. He takes away the sin, the guilt, and the shame of his people. This shuts the mouth of Satan. It takes the power away from his accusations.

But the Lord goes even further. Not only does he strip away the sin of the priest, but he now covers him in "festal robes" and a "clean turban" (Zech 3:4–5). This is a picture of double imputation. My sins were given to Christ on the cross. His righteous record is given to me in the cosmic courtroom of the universe. My moral deficit was imputed to his account. His righteous wealth was deposited into my account. He paid my sin debt. I get his righteous reward!

Some say a good definition of justification in Christian theology is "just as if I had never sinned." That's half true. It's not false; it just leaves half the goodness out. Justification *truly* means "just as if I had never sinned *and* just as if I had committed thirty-three years of righteous deeds!"

When anyone trusts in Christ, their sin record is stripped away eternally. But the sinless, spotless, righteous record of Christ is credited to their account. They are clothed in his royal, righteous robes! Notice that when God speaks, he never mentions Joshua's efforts of good works or sanctification. Joshua is silent and passive. God fights for him. God vindicates and protects. Joshua is silent and enjoys God's work on our behalf. We should do the same. This is an incredible picture of how salvation works.

ACCEPTED

The good news doesn't stop here. Often, we think of the gospel as a blank slate given to us. But that's not true. That's not good enough. If God wiped my slate fully clean today, I would get it dirty and sinful again before bedtime! A clean slate isn't enough.

The judge pronounces us not guilty by the blood of Christ. Then the judge stands, removes his judicial robes, and walks to us. He puts his arm around us. He says, "I heard that you were a child of Satan but that now you're set free. You need a new family. I want to adopt you into my family. Come, let's go home. And I've got a fresh set of clothes for you when we get there."

We will still struggle and sin, stumble and fall. But he loves and accepts us fully, even as he loves and accepts his own eternal Son. It seems too good to be true, but it is 100 percent true. He is never tired of fighting for one of his own!

There are two great dangers when we consider these things. The first is legalism. Legalism can show up in two separate ways. Legalism can drive us to despair because, deep down, we know we will never be good enough. We will never meet the standard of perfection, and thus we are constantly downtrodden and beaten down.

But what many do with legalism is they shrink the standard. They "right-size" the law to fit their performance. Then they work their hardest and feel smug and self-assured. Consequently, they look down their noses at anyone who doesn't agree with or achieve their personal standards. Legalism always leads to pride or despair. There is no middle ground.

The opposite yet equally deadly danger of legalism is licentiousness, or lawlessness. These are the classic grace abusers who, either with their mouths, lives, or both, boldly say, "Jesus died for all my sins so I can sin with impunity. I will have my cake and eat it too. I will party my brains out here on earth in sin and then live with Christ in eternity!"

God's adopting us into his family strikes at both errors. Adoption kills legalism because Christ already met the standard for me. I am in. I don't have to achieve a status; I receive my blood-bought status from the hand of Christ by faith. But adoption likewise attacks lawlessness. We should be so shocked at God's kindness, mercy, and initiation to us that we would never want to sin in ways that would grieve his heart.

Essentially the Father says to us, "I don't want a legal relationship with you but a familial one. Obey me, but I know it won't be perfect in this life. That's why I've clothed you in your big brother Jesus's clothes. But please take killing sin seriously. Fumble forward in faithful service because you love me, like me, and desire to please me."

The Holy Spirit will convict Christians of sin and invite us to repent. At times conviction and condemnation can feel terribly similar and be hard to distinguish. How can we know the difference?

Satan's condemnation is often vague and always hopeless. It seeks to drive us away from God and into our own efforts. Notice that Satan never accused Joshua of a specific sin. It's hard to repent of sin in general. Condemnation is often generic and thus leads to despair. There's nothing we can do except sit around and feel guilty.

The Holy Spirit's conviction is usually extremely specific. It is also filled with hope. He beckons you to confess, repent, and return to your first love. This leads to a restored intimacy with God. Godly sorrow leads to repentance and life. Worldly sorrow leads only to vain personal effort and death (2 Cor 7:10).

APPLICATION

"Christ never performs the work of the priesthood, but that Satan stands at his side, that is, devises all means by which he may remove and withdraw Christ from his office."[7] Even though Christ has lived, died, and risen, Satan still accuses. Satan has not quit. He will still whisper into sinners' minds to heap guilt on them. Satan will fight to the end to wound as many of God's people as he can. He will do all he can to keep us out of any ministry efforts to serve the Lord and others.

"Most of the devil's advantage depends on the ability to move among human affairs undetected."[8] If we are unaware of his attacks, lies, and accusations, we will be more susceptible to give into them as true. Even if we think it's just negative self-talk, we will be likely to try and combat it on our own through more hard work. If we can identify Satan's attacks, hopefully we will be quicker to take these thoughts captive to the gospel and apply grace to ourselves in the right way.

Part of why we struggle so much is we are often so ignorant of Satan's personalized schemes to accuse and condemn us. We must grow to be experts in how Satan personally pursues us so that we can become experts on how God speaks back on our behalf in the exact ways we need. This is a lifelong journey. No one will fully arrive in this life.

CONCLUSION

Verses 8 and 9 seem strange to our modern era, but they would not have to Joshua. The Servant, the Branch, the Stone, these were all prophetic imagery of the coming messiah who would take away all the sin of all God's people in one day. No more days of atonement would be needed! Christians have been saved by Christ once for all (Heb 10:10)!

The ancient high priest who represented all God's people needed to be cleansed, covered, and clothed by the angel of the Lord because of the priest's personal sin. But the true, eternal high priest is the angel of the Lord. He has no need to be covered or cleansed. He stands alone among humanity in his own sinless, spotless righteousness.

On the cross, the Lord Jesus was stripped bare in our place as the perfect Lamb of God. He was offered as the sacrifice for all our filthy sins. He took all our filth on his back so that we might be cleansed and clothed in perfect righteousness!

Kevin DeYoung teaches, "Our Lord Jesus is in heaven pleading our case, so that whenever Satan accuses us in our conscience or dares to lay

---

7. Calvin, *Minor Prophets*, 83.
8. Lovelace, *Dynamics*, 136.

a charge before the Father, Jesus Christ, God's own Son and our flawless advocate, stands ready to defend us and plead His own blood for our sakes. Think about that. Christ is our prayer partner in heaven."[9] What greater help can we ask for!?

Psalm 35:3b says, "Say to my soul, 'I am your salvation.'" It is not enough to intellectually know you are saved. We need to know in the depths of our being that we are saved. We need to feel saved, to feel cleansed. It is so much more powerful when there is a sense that God is personally speaking this truth into your soul. We want this truth and reality to burn and shine in our souls. We need it to overcome the inner accusations of Satan no matter how much truth they may be rooted in.

As you finish this chapter, wherever you are and whatever you are doing, I encourage you to pull out a Bible or pull up the Bible app on your phone. Open to Rom 8. Read the whole chapter slowly. I especially encourage you to read vv. 1–4, 15–17, and 28–39 out loud. Listen as God speaks through his word to your soul personally.

---

9. DeYoung, *We Almost Forgot*, 96.

Chapter 8

Conspiracy of Circumstances

Matthew 4, 16, 27

In this chapter we will see how Satan is an expert in figuring out where we are the weakest and most prone to temptation. Once he has done that, he will relentlessly pursue us, and repeatedly in that same area. He will seek to exploit our weaknesses as ruthlessly as he can. A brief review will be helpful first.

Satan lies and says God isn't good and humans lack something essential. We can't trust God to provide what we need, so we must take matters into our own hands and fix the situation, even if that means sinning to do so.

Adam and Eve bought the lie and bit the forbidden fruit. We have too. Then Satan comes as an accuser and condemner. We feel the depth of our shame and have the right desire to cover it. But we can't truly cover it, though we try. Adam and Eve tried fig leaves, tress, running, hiding, blame shifting, and excuses. None of it worked for them and it won't for us.

What they and we are really trying to do is find a way to deal with the pain and pressure that life on a fallen planet inevitably brings. To the degree we can find legitimate, non-sinful ways to deal with pain and pressure we should. That's wisdom.

If you have terrible back pain and ibuprofen helps, you should take it. God doesn't call Christians to enjoy pain or be stoics with no feelings. But if you decide to get drunk to relieve the pain, you are in sin because Eph 5:18 tells us not to be drunk.

If you are single and overcome with sexual desire and think a cold shower will help, go for it. But if you think the best way to fix the problem is porn, now you're in sin because of what Jesus said in Matt 5:28 about lust. We must only address pain and pressure in life in God-approved ways.

Christians often find subtly sinful ways to avoid the pain and pressure of life. Most of our sinful strategies to deal with life on planet earth aren't as obviously and outwardly scandalous and sinful. We are seeking measures of control, assurance, satisfaction, security, and significance. These are good, God-given desires. But we can seek them in sinful ways.

Lovelace says, "Those who aren't secure in Christ cast about for spiritual life preservers with which to support their confidence, and in their frantic search they cling . . . to the shreds of ability and righteousness they find in themselves. . . . [It] is put on as though it were armor against self doubt . . . and can never be removed except through comprehensive faith in the saving work of Christ."[1]

We are much more nuanced today in our sinful self-protection than Adam and Eve were in the garden. They put their best foot forward, their fear forward, and their excuses forward, but none of it worked.[2] We do the same thing, and this just perpetuates and deepens and complicates our sin.

Hebrews 12:1 speaks of "the sin which so easily entangles us." The sin that so easily entangles me might not be the sin that so easily entangles you. Partially based on our unique personality, upbringing, and life circumstances, we have all learned ways to avoid pain in life. Some of these ways may be sinful. Others may not be. Part of the key to killing sin in your life is to understand the unique ways you are most tempted to sin. Most of us have at least one main way we sin to avoid the pain of life and we need to understand what that is.

Satan personalizes his attacks for each of us. We must personalize our defense and our counter attacks. He roots his lies in enough reality to make them plausible to us. We must become experts on ourselves and experts on his personalized schemes against us. Then, by grace, we must defeat his schemes. We must understand Satan's temptation, repetition, and salvation.

---

1. Lovelace, *Dynamics*, 198, 212.
2. For more on how we do this today, see appendix A.

TEMPTATION

We have already looked at Matt 4 in chapter 4. Satan came against Jesus with three specific temptations rooted in his current reality and experiences. He was all alone and had no food, no friends, no followers, no fame, no fortune. Satan came with quick and easy fixes to address all that Jesus seemed to lack.

The first two temptations didn't seem to bother Jesus much. He rejected them quickly and easily. He brushed past them. The third temptation was different and the most daunting and it did seem to strike a chord with Christ.

He seems to get angry with Satan; he tells him to scram, and Satan does. What was the real temptation and why did it strike such a nerve? It was to skip the cross and get the crown. We know that Christ did not want to go to the cross and that he could have gotten out of it if he wanted to. When Judas and others came to arrest Christ, Christ said he could have asked his Father to send legions of angels to protect him and the Father would have done it (Matt 26:45).

In John 12:31 and 16:11 Jesus refers to Satan as "the ruler of this world." Jesus came back to conquer planet earth and return it to his Father's full authority. We pray for this in the Lord's Prayer. "Your kingdom come. Your will be done, On earth as it is in heaven" (Matt 6:10).

The Father's plan for Jesus to accomplish this was through the suffering and death of Jesus on the cross. Jesus knew this. There was already some dread of the pain that was to come to win the earth back. Satan appealed to that.

If Jesus would bow down to Satan, Satan would give him all the world. He could get all the riches, power, and glory and skip the pain and shame of the cross. It is quite appealing in one sense and understandably so.

Satan likes to come to us early in life and find where we are the weakest and/or most susceptible to his schemes. Satan tells us the way to get our best life now is his way, not God's. John Calvin observes, "All these things, says he, are mine, and it is only through me that they are obtained. We have to contend every day with the same imposture: for every believer feels it in himself. . . . Though we are convinced, that all our support, and aid, and comfort, depend on the blessing of God, yet our senses allure and draw us away, to seek assistance from Satan, as if God alone were not enough."[3] This is incredibly insightful. We know the truth.

---

3. Calvin, *Harmony of the Evangelists*, 220.

CONSPIRACY OF CIRCUMSTANCES

Yet circumstances conspire to tell us to "seek assistance from Satan." This is what we are doing when we knowingly sin to satisfy a desire.

I mentioned earlier a young man with an absentee mom. The lies he heard were "You're not respectable the way you are" and "You must change to have respect." He developed a strategy to deal with it. He tried hard to change and be what those around him wanted him to be so he could earn their respect. He grew up in Christian churches and ministries. So, his strategy to get respect was by being "very spiritual." This often looked good on the outside but was deadly on the inside. He became a people pleaser. And no matter how pleased they were, it was never enough to fulfill his longing for respect.

Here's a wicked little secret Satan and sin won't tell you. Even if you get exactly what you're trying to get through your sinful schemes, it won't satisfy the depths of your soul. It'll be like your breath outside on a freezing day. You glimpse it for a second. Before you can touch it with your hand it's gone.

I mentioned a man named Ted in the previous chapter. He was compared to his older brother in sports and felt like a failure. His lie is, "You're always a failure." His strategy to deal with it is to always hedge his bets. He never swings for the fences. He always plays it safely, swimming too close to the shore in life. He rarely risks in life. Then if things don't go well, he can comfort himself. "I didn't really fail. I just didn't try my best."

I know another man whose strategy is to joke about everything. Nothing is serious. He is hilarious, and this is how he deals with the pain, the shame, and the pressure of life. There are plenty of fun things in life we should joke about. But there are also serious things that we should be sober minded about, such as our sin. If we begin to joke about even our sinful shortcomings in life, this is an unhealthy way to deal with the pain and pressure of life.

I know another man who just stays shallow. He is so reluctant and hesitant to talk about anything below the surface. He's been hurt by people. He is tender. But he acts like nothing bothers him. He acts like it's all OK with him. Nothing is a big deal, not even his wounds. This can lead him to never want to talk about his own sin and struggles. Not talking about sin is a strategy to ignore the pain, but in truth, it perpetuates the sin and extends the pain eventually.

Another woman grew up with an alcoholic father. She became an expert in reading his mood, over the phone or each time she walked in the door. She could tell if he was drunk or not. If he was drunk, she avoided him at all costs. Now, as an adult, she is always scanning the horizon for any sign of danger or pain. And if she sees or smells anything that says danger to her, she makes quick plans to avoid it at all costs. It's not wrong to be aware of danger. It is wrong to live in perpetual fear, worry, and anxiety.

The last example brings up an important point. We often develop these strategies to avoid pain early in life. And often, they are not sinful when we first develop them. They are the best we can do as immature children. An elementary aged girl learning to go to her room and lock her door when her dad is drunk isn't sinful; she's wise. She shouldn't be condemned for that.

But here's the danger. As she matures, what was an understandable strategy for a young girl can become a sinful strategy for an adult Christian. Her strategy of "Detect potential pain and avoid it at all costs" won't work well later in life.

Imagine she marries a husband who struggles with depression. She comes home from work and senses he's in a bad mood. She immediately goes upstairs to watch TV and ignores him for the rest of the night to protect herself from the pain of a long, hard conversation. It's understandable but it's not loving. How should a godly wife respond to a husband who's struggling and down in the dumps? She should pursue him, love him, comfort him, speak the truth to him, and listen to him.

But if over a twenty-year period she's developed a strategy that is a knee jerk reaction at this stage of life—"Avoid all pain at all costs"—she'll be unable to love him the way God calls her to. She will subtly be rejecting God's plan for her life and pursuing Satan's although the roots of this strategy are very innocent.

Another woman I know was mistreated as a child. She was a victim. No one helped her. It was tragic. Now she is an adult Christian. The problem is, anytime something goes wrong in her life, she still tells herself and others, "This is not my fault. I am the victim." Sometimes that is true, sometimes it is not. She has made some horrible financial decisions, sinful decisions. But she refuses to take responsibility for her financial difficulties. She acts as though someone else made her waste her money.

The woman in the previous chapter I called Lynn learned to be a perfectionist as a child in a broken home. Again, that was a young child trying their best to survive. But as an adult the pressure to get everything exactly right can be overwhelming and even damning if it is not repented of.

We can identify how others do this. I hope that we can see how we sinfully protect ourselves. These strategies start young in life and then become locked into our normal ways of thinking. Though they are clearly sinful later in life, they can be very hard to repent of because they have worked so well for us for so long.

Imagine you were on a boat that was destroyed in a storm. You clung to a broken piece of wood to survive the waves and the wind. Two days later you are clinging for dear life to the piece of wood that kept you afloat. The Coast Guard finds you. You are overjoyed, and they want to pull you into their boat. They tell you that you must let go of the piece of wood. You say that you can't. Your fingernails are dug into the wood so deep. Your fists are locked onto it. You have a psychological connection to it because it got you through the storm and kept you alive.

The Coast Guard captain says that he understands. But he also warns you. "I know that piece of wood saved your life last night. But now it's killing you. It is covered in barnacles, and they are cutting you. You are bleeding. If you stay here, you will slowly bleed to death, or the sharks will get you. You've got to let go of the wood and come into the boat."

We all may have developed non-sinful strategies as kids to deal with the pain, shame, and pressure of life. But as adults they often become sinful and slowly start to kill us and ruin our lives. We must learn to let go of these old strategies and climb fully into the boat of Christ.

REPETITION

We have no record that Satan ever tempted Jesus with breaking a fast early a second time or turning rocks into bread again. That temptation didn't seem to gain any traction. But the temptation to skip the cross and get the crown does come back around. Imagine you are a boxer and learn that your opponent has a broken left lower rib. If you are wise, you'll do all you can to hit that same rib repeatedly from every different angle you can. This is what Satan does to us.

In Matt 16:21 Jesus begins to teach the disciples that he must go to Jerusalem, suffer, and die. Peter is no dummy. If Jesus is the Messiah and Peter is his trusted assistant, Jesus's suffering will include Peter's suffering. Peter wants no part in that. Peter is sinfully trying to avoid the pain of life; the life God has called him to. But he may not have even realized he was doing it at first. He may have thought that he was just trying to help his friend have a more positive view of the future.

Peter pulls Jesus aside to tell him not to talk that way. "Stop with all this negative self-talk Lord. You're not going to suffer and die!" Jesus is wise to see how Satan is using his friend Peter to bring the same old lie and temptation up again in a different time, way, and place. He rebukes Peter strongly. "Get behind me, Satan! You are a stumbling block to Me" (Matt 16:23).

Matthew Henry is helpful. "It is the subtlety of Satan, to send temptations to us by the unsuspected hands of our best and dearest friends. Even the kindness of our friends are often abused by Satan, and made use of as temptation to us. We should learn to know the devil's voice when he speaks in a saint as well as when he speaks in a serpent."[4]

The man I've mentioned before who grew up with an absentee mom ended up with a very cold and critical friend group. All the lies he heard through his relationship with his mom were reinforced later in life by his friends. Satan does not play fair. He never shows mercy. He is evil incarnate.

The man may switch his strategy at times. Sometimes he may try his best to be a perfect friend and earn his friend's respect. It doesn't work and he can't sustain it. So, he may swing the pendulum to the other side. "I'm not changing anything for you. If you can't respect me just the way I am, that's your problem!" This doesn't work either. The problem is that these are both sinful, self-centered strategies to fight against the pain and pressure of life rather than Christ-centered strategies to fight against the lies of Satan. He should seek to grow in Christ to be the best friend he can be to please Christ. This is the biblical, balanced approach. But our sinful strategies send us to extremes to keep us from such wisdom.

The man I've mentioned before and called Ted heard lies that started with a football coach: "Why can't you be more like your older brother?" Later in life, his first job assignment was a tough one and didn't go well. It was no fault of his; his bosses put him in a tough place. But the old lie is reinforced, "You are a failure." He too has duel man-centered strategies to fight these lies.

The first is the strategy of apathy. To put a God-centered spin on it, he might call it God-centered passivity. He says to himself, "God is in control so I can rest. I don't have to work that hard. If I don't get the job done, someone else will. It's not a big deal." Much of that is true and sounds good. Remember Satan is an expert in rooting lies in truth. And

---

4. Henry, *Commentary*, 88.

Satan is often the one suggesting to us the sinful strategies to fight against the sinful lies he's telling us. He attacks us in both ways.

What this man is really saying on the inside to himself is "I just won't try hard at anything. I'll act like I don't care much. Then, when and if I fail, it won't hurt so badly. I won't look so bad. And I can tell myself and others, 'Well, if I really would've tried my best, I would've accomplished the goal, but I was taking it easy, so you really can't evaluate me this time.'"

This man is a Christian, and he knows that it's sinful to use God's sovereignty as an excuse to not work hard for God's glory. At some point he'll get convicted, overwhelmed, or called out by someone. The danger then is he can swing the pendulum to the opposite, yet simultaneously sinful, extreme.

If his first strategy is apathy, his second strategy is anxiety. Now the burden is fully on his back. He is alone and crushed by all he has put off and procrastinated on. Now, he feels hyper-stretched, burdened, and responsible. It's all up to him. If he doesn't come through, he really will be a failure. This can become anxiety producing in so many ways.

If the first strategy is passivity in God's name, this one is a man-centered activity. Again, both of his strategies are sinful although they may contain much truth. These are personalized false gospels. "If I work hard enough, then I'll succeed and I'll no longer be a failure!"

All of us are doing this to a degree. We hear and/or feel the whisper of Satan's personalized lies and accusations in our minds. Then our knee-jerk reaction is to come up with a personalized strategy to fight back against this lie. We either accept it and essentially say, "I am a loser, a failure, unloved etc. . . . There's nothing I can do about it. I might as well just accept it." Or we try in all our own strength to fight it. "I am not a loser. I never fail. I am loved! I will work hard and prove myself and show the world how great, worthy, and accomplished I am." Both strategies will end in failure.

The truth is often in the middle of our two strategies. Think about the man who felt disrespected by his friends. It can seem spiritual to say, "God loves me the way I am, so I'll be content with the way I am and never change." But the truth is that God loves us despite how sinful we are and because he loves us so much, he desperately wants us to change and grow up and out of our sinful behavior.

For the man, if anxiety and apathy are both bad strategies, what's the right response? A God-centered activity. Christians should work hard as unto the Lord but should do so in a complete spirit and attitude of trust and dependence. If the Lord doesn't bless the work of my hands, I fail (Ps 127:1–2). Apart from Christ, we can do nothing (John 15:5). But with him, I can accomplish all he desires me to (Phil 4:13).

Part of what it truly means to trust in Christ is to embrace the pain and sorrow that comes from obeying him. Mature Christians should be willing to suffer pain and pressure in this life to stay pure, holy, undefiled, and faithful to him. We refuse to seek sinful ways to self-medicate, isolate, and sedate. In Matt 16:24–25 Jesus said, "If anyone wishes to come after Me, let him deny himself, and take up his cross, and follow Me. For whoever wishes to save his life shall lose it; but whoever loses his life for My sake shall find it." Don't try to preserve your quality of life in sinful ways. Be willing to lose it for Christ to gain it in the end. I have a friend and mentor who says, "Embrace the sorrow." The idea is to know there will be pain in the Christian life; don't be surprised or angry when it comes, and don't try to avoid it in sinful ways.

SALVATION

What Satan is offering to all of us in diverse ways is a way to save ourselves. He calls us to save ourselves from the pain and pressure of life and to do it apart from Christ. We must refuse his attractive offer. Satan will relentlessly pursue us with this enticing offer. He will show up in the worst of times and temptations. We must see past his enticing bait and notice the deadly hook.

Matthew 27 tells us of Jesus's death. In v. 34 as they prepare to nail him to the cross, he is offered a drink mixed with gall. Almost certainly it had some type of narcotic effect. Crucifixion was one of the most painful ways to die. Some prisoners would freak out as they suffered hours on end. The numbing effect of this drink might calm them slightly for the long hours of torture they were to endure. The intent may have been to make it easier to get criminals to lay down and stretch out on the cross so the soldiers could fasten them to the cross with terribly long, railroad-spike-like nails.

When Jesus tasted it and realized what it was, he refused to drink it. He wanted to have his mind fully engaged as he suffered for his people. He was wise to know that Satan's attacks would continue on the cross. The lies would continue to come from new angles when Christ was at his

CONSPIRACY OF CIRCUMSTANCES

worst and lowest physically, mentally, and emotionally. He had to do all he could to fight the fight of faith for us.

He wanted to be fully sober and focused. He wanted to face God's plan for his life, eyes wide open. It was not easy or fun. But he chose to lose his life so that he might save our lives.

Verses 39 and 40 indicate that as random strangers passed by on the road and saw Christ, they mocked him. But listen to what they specifically said, "Save Yourself! If You are the Son of God, come down from the cross" (Matt 27:39–40). "If You are the Son of God." This sounds so like Satan's direct temptation in Matt 4. "Come down from the cross" sounds terribly similar to the message Peter spoke in Matt 16. He essentially said, "Don't go to the cross!"

Satan will find the temptation that is the most powerful to you personally and then he will attack you in diverse kinds of ways and places, with different thoughts, people, and voices. Be aware. Be on the lookout.

Verses 41 through 43 show the chief priests, scribes, and elders saying something remarkably similar. They insinuate that if God really were his Father, if God really loved him, he would save him. God the Father would protect Christ if Christ was really his Son. Satan will whisper this same lie into the minds of believers. Satan will orchestrate circumstances and relationships in our life to convince us that God doesn't love us at all, just like he did against Job.

Verse 44 shows that even the criminals crucified with him delivered the same message to Christ. Where in your life have you felt like circumstances and even people are conspiring to convince you that God doesn't love you and won't do what's best for you. Be on your guard when you sense this feeling rises in your soul.

Satan has no mercy. He will find where you are weakest and orchestrate his attacks through various people and events to drive a wedge between you and your Father in heaven. Calvin states,

> And whenever God does not assist us according to our wish, but conceals his aid for a little time, it is a frequent stratagem of Satan, to allege that our hope was to no purpose, as if his promise failed. . . . This . . . is a very sharp arrow of temptation which Satan holds in his hand, when he pretends God has forgotten us, because He does not relieve us speedily. . . . Satan, therefore, attempts to drive us to despair by this logic, that it is vain for

us to feel assured of the love of God, when we do not clearly perceive his aid.[5]

Listen to Calvin's wisdom. Anytime we feel that God has abandoned us or not answered our prayers, we are very susceptible to Satan's schemes. Anytime we feel that God could or should be doing more to protect us or provide for us or promote us, we are in danger of believing Satan's lies about God's character.

When we are in a season where we feel like God is far from us, this temptation strikes the hardest. When God does not act like we would like or expect, we are in danger. And God often does not function as we would like or expect!

This lie is so like the lie of Satan in the garden. God is not enough. God isn't doing enough for you. So, take care of yourself. Take matters into your own hands, even if you must break rules in the process. Protect yourself. Vindicate yourself! Rise up!

David is a classic example of the right way to respond. Two chapters, 1 Sam 24 and 26, tell the story of David's trusting God's ways rather than sinful strategies to protect himself. Two times that we know of David had a chance to kill crazy King Saul. David could've saved himself by killing the man trying to kill him. One time Saul came into a cave alone where David was hiding. Circumstances made it too easy! His men urged David to kill Saul. At least once one man offered to kill Saul for David. So much temptation to sinfully protect himself battered David. But he stood strong by grace. And we must as well. How did he do it? He trusted God to fight his battles for him, protect him, vindicate him, and make all things right in his life eventually, in God's own way and timing. So often our timetable doesn't align with the Lord's, and this is where we can get in the most trouble.

APPLICATION

We need to consider ways that we can recognize our own tendencies to protect or to vindicate ourselves in sinful ways. How does Satan tempt you to provide for yourself or promote yourself in ways that won't honor or please God? When you finish reading this chapter it would be great to talk to those that know you best, a best friend and/or mentor. Ask them how they see you trying to guard yourself against the pain and pressure

---

5. Calvin, *Harmony of the Evangelists*, 3:304, 306.

of life in ways that may not be sinful at first glance. But upon further investigation these strategies may have sinful roots.

I'll share part of my own story and struggle. I think God has gifted me to preach and teach his word. I've been doing it for over thirty years now. That's a good thing. Even before that, my parents and others told me I should be a lawyer because I could argue so well. I'm not sure this was a compliment!

Telling the truth is a wonderful thing. But it can also be weaponized in sinful ways to protect myself. For example, if I start to feel the pain and pressure of life from my wife or one of my children or someone I work with, ruthless truth telling can become a defense mechanism. It can become a brushback pitch that says, "You don't want to cross me. You don't want to mess with me, or I can hurt you with my words and the truth. So back off!"

Imagine someone is giving me constructive criticism that is right and I need to hear. But for whatever reason, I'm in a bad mood or I'm sensitive about the specific issue they are bringing up. So, I don't want to hear it, at least not right now. How might I respond?

I can go on the attack. I can drop into a cold, hard, rational-lawyer mode. I can move into the attitude of a drill sergeant. "Oh, you want to question me? Do you want to attack and criticize me? Well, you're not perfect. I've been keeping a secret record of mistakes in my mind of all the ways you've been failing lately. So let me just share some of those with you. Tit for tat."

Now, I'm not quite stupid or arrogant enough to say it just like that. I'm a little more sly and subtle. But this expresses my sinful heart attitude at times. I can dress it up with a smile and a gentle tone and spiritual words. But the effect can be similar. Cross me at your own risk, because I can make you pay if you push too far.

This is wickedness. This is selfish. This is fear based. I'm not trusting God. I ought to trust God enough to speak hard truth to me through other Christians! I ought to invite it and take it, humbly and eagerly.

Telling the truth is a good and right thing, in itself. But it can also be weaponized as a form of sinful self-protection. My example above should make that clear. Then what should I do?

I should accept my cross, deny myself, and follow Christ and be willing to lose my life, security, reputation, comfort, pride, and sense of safety (Matt 16:24–25 // Luke 9:23–24). Jesus teaches us to lose our life in the short run to gain it overall. How does that apply here?

Don't try to sinfully save your life. Don't try to sinfully save your reputation. Don't try and sinfully protect yourself from hard and awkward conversations, circumstances, or situations.

Life is painful, one way or the other. We often choose what type of pain we will suffer though. Suffer the pain of eating healthy and going to the gym, or suffer the pain of being overweight and unhealthy. We face similar choices in so much of life. I can suffer the short-term pain of listening to constructive criticism that is hard to hear and thus grow more mature. Or I can ignore it, protect myself, and suffer the pain of spiritual stagnation.

If I can learn to shut up, humble myself, listen to others, give them the benefit of doubt, and stay focused and present, I will learn helpful things about myself. If I can keep my guard down, my facial expression warm, my body language calm, my tone of voice tender, I should be able to ask clarifying questions in a non-defensive way and come away with helpful insight about myself. It may feel very painful in the moment, like being operated on without anesthesia. But, just like a helpful surgery, it can make me much happier and healthier eventually.

For me, when someone is giving me feedback, I must focus on not nitpicking them to death. Even if much of what they say is unfair or untrue, if I am wise, I will learn to search for the needle of truth in the haystack of error. This is never an enjoyable process. It is an incredibly rewarding one though, when done well.

If I have sinned against someone or hurt them, I can and should acknowledge that, apologize, and ask for forgiveness. Again, this can be painful in the moment to humble myself. But it can lead to a deeper, more enjoyable life with better, more reconciled relationships.

When I was twenty-two and newly married, I didn't see any of this about myself. I was very self-righteous and arrogant. My attitude was, "My job is to speak the hard truth. Your job, the listener (my sweet wife!), is to take it and deal with it." It didn't make for a great marriage.

Below the surface, I didn't like being criticized by anyone, and certainly not by my wife. Especially because I thought for every sin she could accuse me of, I could easily accuse her of two or three. I did not speak the truth in love. My "truth speaking" was a sinful form of self-protection and self-promotion. You could even say in it was a false gospel. I was hiding my sin and shame behind my verbal attacks and defenses. I didn't think I was going to heaven because of my ruthless truth telling. I did think I could carve out a little slice of "heaven on earth" with my truth telling. I could protect my reputation. And if my wife would just listen and agree, we could have a great, peaceful marriage as well. My sinful self-protection almost ruined our marriage. We fought like cats and dogs. I deeply hurt my wife with my words. My weaponized truth telling didn't pull my wife out of her sinful patterns. It pushed her deeper into sin and insecurity and worry. It also drove her further away from me.

What I wanted was a close, intimate, comfortable marriage. What I got was a distant, cold, hard marriage. Often when we pursue a good thing in a sinful way, we will actually be pushing ourselves further from the good thing we were pursuing. Satan's schemes never work out well overall.

How in your life do you tend to sinfully protect yourself? How do you tend to sinfully promote yourself? Where do you provide for yourself or please yourself in a way that is not according to God's standard?

CONCLUSION

Satan tempted Jesus with sinful strategies to escape the pain and pressure of life on planet earth. But Christ resisted them all. As Christ hung on the cross suffering for the sins of his people, he never once responded directly to all his critics, mockers, tempters, and tormentors. He didn't even command Satan to depart, though he must have known Satan was behind so much of the mockery and temptation. Rather, he turned to his Father and prayed the psalms of David.

He quoted Ps 22. He essentially prayed, "Where are you, Father? Why aren't you with me? Why aren't you helping me and vindicating me in this moment?!" He wrestled honestly with his Father in prayer. He poured out all the woes of his heart to a God that, at that moment, felt eternally distant. This is a great pattern for us. He knew the truth and yet was honest with God about his feelings, pain, suffering, and experience in that moment.

One thing we should notice is that when Jesus prayed in Matt 27:46, he didn't call God "Father." He merely called out, "My God, My God." In that moment he didn't feel like God was his Father. He was not experiencing the goodness of his Father but rather the terror of wrath of the Judge.

Over forty times in Matthew's gospel, Jesus referred to God as Father. He intentionally used this term of intimacy, warmth, love, and closeness. Matthew 27:46, in some sense, is a cry of abandonment. In another sense it is a cry of hope. He still calls him "My God."

Our foolish strategies to save and protect ourselves never ultimately work, though they may seem to be helpful in the short run. They always ultimately backfire and make our lives worse. We must be aware of this.

Christ could have protected himself that day. Christ could have come down from the cross if he had genuinely wanted to. He could have skipped the cross altogether. He could have saved himself. But if he did that, he would not have been able to save us.

"Hell came to Calvary that day, and the Savior descended into it and bore its horrors in our stead."[6] Jesus was willing to lose his life for us. He was willing to embrace and experience all the pain and pressure of literal hell on earth that we might reign one day in paradise with him!

So, when he calls us to lay down our lives and suffer a little pain and pressure in the short term, we should not flinch back. For his will and glory, we should gladly embrace the pain of following him. If we are living for the joy set before us, we will be able to rest in him.

He endured the cross for the joy set before him (Heb 12:3). He has set joy before us in heaven that we might endure, trusting him. The joy is that we will be with him for all eternity! He will vindicate us at the proper time. He will eternally protect us. He is protecting us now. We can rest in and with him. We should rejoice in him! By grace, we will live for him. Hallelujah! What a Savior!

---

6. Hendriksen, *Matthew*, 970.

Chapter 9

Forgiven to Be Free

Ephesians 4, 6

Holy living flows out of knowing, believing, loving, and embracing truth with your whole life. Sin flows from believing, loving, and embracing lies. Before someone comes to Christ, the person is fully sinful. They are deceived spiritually, enslaved to lies and falsehood. Once glorified in Christ in eternity, we will be fully holy, right with God, living in truth all the time. When someone comes to Christ but still lives in this fallen world, they are a mixed work. Sin still lives in them though it does not reign. The Holy Spirit lives in them as well, but he does not exert total influence over all they say, think, do, and feel at this point. Christians are tempted to use sinful strategies to deal with the pain and pressure of life.

Satan is still real and active. Once someone is saved, Satan doesn't admit defeat and give up. If anything, he ramps up his activity. The five main people we see Satan clearly come after in the Bible, that we have examined in this book, are Adam, Eve, Job, Jesus, and Peter. Two sinless people in Eden, the godliest man on the earth in his day, the God man himself, and Jesus's number one disciple. The more you seek to follow God, the more Satan will attack.

Satan continues to lie to us. We are not immune to it. We still must put off the psychology of the old life we had before we were Christians.[1] Revelation 12:9 tells us that Satan deceives the entire world. He doesn't play fairly. He often starts when people are young and before they've become Christians. He uses people we know and love and trust to lie to

---

1. Ferguson, *Whole*, 121.

us; people such as parents, siblings, extended family, friends, teachers, coaches, bosses, and more.

Lloyd-Jones has a helpful reminder for us:

> You will be engaged in a terrible conflict with the devil and all his forces. If you do not realize that . . . and take appropriate action with respect to it, you will undoubtedly and inevitably be defeated. . . . The devil does work in us and can work in us through our bodies, through our instincts. The devil can make use of anything. I must never think that my whole problem is confined to that which is within me and in other people. Much teaching concerning holiness and sanctification never even mentions the devil and these powers at all. . . . Hence the total inadequacy of many proposed solutions. . . . Subtlety is the great characteristic of the devil. . . . He uses it most of all by attacking man in the realm of his mind. . . . The devil is constantly trying to insinuate doubts into our minds. . . . It is often very difficult to control our mind and thoughts and imaginations. The devil has power to lead them, and especially if you are not aware of it and fail to stop them. And thus he will take you captive, and make you intensely miserable. . . . There is nothing . . . which is more significant about evangelicalism in this present century than the way in which it has largely ignored this teaching concerning the devil . . . and the "wiles" of the devil. . . . The devil wears a mask. . . . He is an actor who appears in different characters.[2]

There is a grave danger of assuming all your problems, sins, and struggles have natural roots. Some may. Some don't. Satan is hunting you. It may not be Satan himself but one of his demons doing his work.

Satan used Adam's passivity to lead Eve to sin. He used Eve to tempt Adam to sin. He used Job's wife to encourage Job to curse God. He used Peter and random people walking past the cross—priests, elders, and thieves—to try and lead Jesus to leave the cross.

Who has Satan used in your life to lie to you about God, about yourself, about what is genuinely good, and about the gospel? Hopefully, you've been thinking about that as you've read this book, and as I've shared different stories and examples from the Bible and modern-day life. The main lie for you may have first been insinuated over forty years ago. Maybe you heard it loud and clear in your mind last week. More likely it has been a doubt or an accusation that you have heard repeated over and over in various times, ways, and places for most of your life, like

---

2. Lloyd-Jones, *Christian Warfare*, 15, 17, 19, 83, 85–86, 89, 98, 103.

we saw in the life of Christ. What is the main temptation you face most often? Your lie certainly lies near that temptation.

To the degree we still believe the lie, we give it power in our lives. One of the clearest pieces of evidence that we still subtly believe Satan's lies and accusations is when we refuse to forgive those who have hurt us. Especially when we refuse to forgive those through whom the lie has come. This is one of Satan's most powerful, insidious, effective, and yet subtle schemes. He uses it to keep many enslaved to sin and to his lies for a lifetime.

SATAN'S CHANCE

Ephesians 4:26 is not a command as much as it is a concession: "Be angry, and yet do not sin; do not let the sun go down on your anger." Paul knows there is such a thing as godly anger. He also knows it is dangerous. If you get righteously angry over something but hold on to that anger too long, it can quickly and easily turn into sinful anger. It festers and grows sinfully stale. In v. 31 of the same chapter, five short verses away, he instructs us to get rid of all anger. Most human anger is sinful (Jas 1:19–20) and even when we have righteous anger, be careful! It can turn on you so quickly!

If you're angry, check to see if it's sinful or not. Are you mad at sin? That's good. Or are you just angry for selfish reasons? That's a sin. Repent of sinful anger quickly. But even with godly anger, deal with it quickly as well so that it doesn't metastasize into something much worse. Treat righteous anger like the proverbial hot potato. Get rid of it ASAP! Human beings aren't made to hold on to anger for too long. It will burn us up from the inside out.

Anger is a gateway sin that often leads to worse sin, including murder (Matt 5:21–22). You don't have to deal with it before nightfall. If you live at the North Pole, that obviously doesn't mean you get months to deal with anger in the summer when night never comes but must deal with it instantly in winter when night has always fallen! The point is to deal with it as soon as you realistically can. Don't stow it away for later. Don't procrastinate and put it off indefinitely.

Ephesians 4:27 tells us why: "And do not give the devil an opportunity." The verse is straight forward but I wonder if we have really considered the depths of what's happening here. Do you understand what is said?

We are warned. F. F. Bruce says, "Let reconciliation be effected before nightfall. . . . If that is not possible . . . then at least the heart should be unburdened of its animosity by the committal of the matter to God . . . 'nursing one's wrath to keep it warm' is not recommended as a wise policy. . . . It magnifies the grievance, makes reconciliation more difficult . . . and the prime promoter and exploiter of such discord is the devil."[3] If you can't deal with it ASAP with the person for whatever reason, at least deal with it ASAP in your heart by prayer. Ask God to help you to forgive, to want to forgive. Entrust the matter of vindication and protection to him. John MacArthur teaches, "Dealing with demons in one's Christian life is . . . being committed to the spiritual means of grace that purifies the soul, so that there is no unclean place that demons could occupy or by which they might gain advantage."[4] He is certainly not some extreme charismatic looking for a demon under every rock, but the Bible is so clear in its teaching here it cannot be ignored. Ignore it at your own peril.

My experience is that the longer we put off dealing with a situation the likelihood grows that we never will. Does this seem true in your life? When you put off healing a conflict does it tend to get better on its own? Does it get easier to deal with later? Often not, because so often it grows as it simmers. Or we harden even as the conflict may cool. We can be complacent in our anger, which may have turned to hate. I spoke with a man recently who is in his seventies. He would say he had a hard relationship with his dad from age five until his dad died. I told him he should forgive his dad. He said, "I don't know if I can. That's too intimidating because I've built up so many psychological self-defenses that it would be too hard to tear them down to deal with dad. I'm still not ready to be vulnerable with my dad." His dad has been dead for years. His dad can't hurt him anymore. And yet, his anger at and/or hurt from his dad has become a part of who he is. He identifies with the pain and hurt so much he can't seem to let go of it and truly forgive. This is how unforgiveness can mark, change, and even define you if you let it. Our wounds can become walls that keep us imprisoned to the hurt we've experienced.[5]

Calvin teaches that we can learn "not to cherish wrath too long in our minds, or allow it sufficient time to become strong. . . . Paul's intention was, to guard us against allowing Satan to take possession of our minds . . . to do whatever he pleases. . . . Instead of resisting the devil, we

---

3. Bruce, *Epistles to the Colossians*, 361.
4. MacArthur, *Ephesians*, 332, 339, 341.
5. Shirmer, *Freedom Fight*, 153.

yield up to him the possession of our heart? Before the poison of hatred has found its way into the heart, anger must be thoroughly dislodged."[6] Notice his strong language. By holding on to anger we allow "Satan to take possession of our minds . . . to do whatever he pleases." The fight against holding grudges is so important.

John Stott is helpful as well. Satan "loves to lurk round angry people, hoping to be able to exploit the situation to his own advantage by provoking them into hatred or violence or a breach of fellowship."[7] Sinful anger opens a door to your heart and invites Satan to come in and have a field day.

And lastly, Warren Wiersbe agrees. "When [Satan] finds a believer with the spark of anger in his heart, he fans those sparks, adds fuel to the fire, and does a great deal of damage to God's people."[8] I want us to see how dangerous this sin can be to ourselves and to all of those around us.

In the same context, Eph 4:30 instructs us not to "grieve the Holy Spirit of God." Matthew Poole says that when we grieve the Spirit, we "make him draw his comfortable presence away from us."[9] God hates all sin. He especially hates it when we hold on to anger at those who have wronged us. This is so antithetical to the gospel and how he has loved and forgiven us!

So, what is the best way to manage righteous anger? What must we do with sinful anger? Forgive "each other, just as God in Christ has also forgiven you" (Eph 4:32).

STAND FIRM

I know this is much easier said than done. Forgiveness is often not easy or natural. It often is not a one-step process we can oversee one day in prayer with God. It can often be complicated and messy, based on what was done or said. How often we were sinned against, extenuating circumstances, and context all play a role in the depth of the sin and thus the depth of the hurt and thus the depth of the forgiveness required to be free.

But the bottom line is we are commanded to forgive when others have sinned against us. Sinful anger invites Satan into the center of our

---

6. Calvin, *Ephesians*, 298–99.
7. Stott, *Ephesians*, 187.
8. Wiersbe, *Be Rich*, 124.
9. Poole, *Commentary on the Whole Bible*, 3:674.

life. It also pushes the Holy Spirit away. Forgiveness pleases the Spirit and stiff arms Satan so that he runs from us. Forgiveness is a way to resist Satan so he will flee from us (Jas 4:7).

Satan's main scheme is to drive a wedge between people and God. His second scheme is to drive a wedge between believers. Often in driving one believer further from another he also drives us further from God, in our hate.

Do you remember the game Red Rover from when you were a child? A line of kids stand hand in hand, grasping on to one another as tightly as they can. They sing to another, similar line of children, "Red Rover, Red Rover, send ____ right over!" In the blank spot they put another child's name who stands in the opposite line of kids, such as John. If they call John with the song, he has to run as fast and hard as he can to run through the opposing line of children. The goal is to find the weak link and run straight at those hands grasped together so that when he hits their hands with his body their hands lose their grip of each other. If he does so, he wins that round. If they are able to maintain their grasp, then John loses.

In a similar fashion Christians are supposed to be tightly united in our relationships with one another. Sinful anger leads to a weakening. Satan loves to try to break our bond, experientially, with one another. Our true bond in Christ can never be broken. Our relationship here on earth can be. This weakens our strength in Christ when there are such divisions in God's church.

Remember, sin didn't just separate Adam and Eve from God. It separated them from each other. Satan's attacks to separate Job from God also brought tension to his marriage. Satan's attacks on Christ through Peter brought pain into that relationship as well.

"Stand firm against the devil. For our struggle is not against flesh and blood" (Eph 6:11–12). Why this warning, reminder, and exhortation? Because so often Satan's schemes are mediated through flesh-and-blood people. Paul reminds us humans are not our real enemy. Satan is.

The people who sinned against you in the past and present and hurt you deeply are not your real enemies. Satan is. The people were pawns. They may have been willing pawns. They may continue to be evil pawns. And yet they are not the ultimate evil. Even if you can fully defeat their scheme in this life, that will not fix all your problems. Your real problem is much deeper.

In college ministry and premarriage counseling I hear so many stories of parents that did evil and abusive things to their children. These deeds, words, and abandonments have warped the way their children now view God, themselves, life, and the gospel. But these adult children are still commanded to forgive the parents who sinned against them.

One of the things that most often helps them to forgive is to better understand how Satan has worked in their parents' lives. The sin and suffering that happened to their parents makes them seem more human and less like evil incarnate. Often, they are only normal sinners trying to survive the pain and pressure of their life just like we all are. They weren't sadists who enjoyed inflicting pain. They weren't Hitler.

More than once, I've heard about emotionally absent fathers who never spent time with a child or never told the child that he loved him or her. Often it comes out later that the grandfather was a drunk who beat his child (the one who is a father now). This father was never taught how to be a dad. He's doing the best he can. The fact that he doesn't hit his children with violence is a win. It doesn't excuse him for being emotionally absent. It does make it more understandable.

This doesn't negate the sin or the responsibility of being a good parent. But when you understand someone else's story, it can make you so much more compassionate and empathetic. One of Satan's main schemes is to keep the pattern of sin, hurt, suffering, blaming, and excuse making going. Don't let him! Let God use you to break generational patterns of sin in your family's line!

God's plan to fight back is forgiveness. We must trust him and obey whether we feel like it or not. I've heard it said, "Forgiveness is a choice before it's a feeling." That's often true. Choose to forgive and pray the feelings come later.

Another thing I will say sometimes to a student I'm mentoring is this: "I've never met your parents. I'm not primarily concerned for them right now. I'm honestly not thinking about them at all right now. I'm thinking about you. I want what's best for you. And what's best for you is to forgive your dad, not for his sake but for yours. I want you to be free of anger, rage, bitterness, etc."

"Those who refuse to forgive continually pick at an open wound, never allowing it to heal. . . . They become tortured prisoners of the offenses and the offender."[10] Bitterness is the poison pill you take and then

---

10. MacArthur, *Luke*, 42.

wait for the other person to die. They may not even know you're angry! We may or may not be hurting them while we nurse our anger. But we are always hurting ourselves when we intentionally hold on to anger. When we keep replaying their deeds and words in our minds, we are allowing those things to define us and shape us. This is Satan's scheme to keep us practically enslaved to sin. He wants to keep his lies, accusations, and doubts warm, powerful, and fruitful for evil in our lives forever, or at least as long as possible.

SHIELD OF FAITH

If someone really wants to move forward in seeking forgiveness, it can be complicated and messy. I won't be able to fully explain it here. There are helpful resources out there if you want to go deeper on this topic.[11]

I will give a brief outline here to point you in the right direction. Forgiveness starts with the heart. You must first pray and ask God to give you a heart willing to forgive. Ask for your desire to forgive to grow. You can pray, "I want to be willing to at least offer forgiveness to the one who has hurt me."

I had a friend who had been sinned against terribly by a brother. He held a grudge against him. I asked him if he would commit to forgiving his brother in the next three months. He said, "No. But I will commit to praying that I can forgive him." That's a great start. Three months later he had reconciled with his brother. It started with his brother repenting. There is such power in humble and honest prayer!

We see this type of heart most clearly with Christ on the cross. In Luke 23:34 he prayed, "Father, forgive them." This must be our starting point as well. At least pray for the good of your enemies. We should want what's best for our enemies. We should desire mercy for them from God and from us! As I persevere in prayer for them, a yearning and longing to forgive should begin to grow in my heart, be it ever so small.

Often in this early stage, we will wonder what will happen if we forgive them. Will this make us drop our guard around them? Will this lead them to erase all boundaries we have erected to protect ourselves? Not necessarily. It is not loving for us to make it easy for them to sin against us in any way they want. We should not encourage them to sin. But the

---

11. For practical considerations on the process of forgiveness, see Keller, *Forgive*; Stubbs, *Forgiveness*; for multiple podcast recordings on forgiveness, see Truth Wars on the PodBean (https://gospeltalk.podbean.com/category/forgiveness).

main thing to remember at this point is God will fight your battles for you. He will protect you. He will vindicate you. David was tempted to kill King Saul because King Saul was trying to kill him. David refused to do so because it would have been sinful. God ordained that Saul would die in battle, and David later became king. God fought David's battles for him, protecting David from sinful self-protection that can come through holding a grudge.

If the person you are seeking to forgive is still in your life and still has potential to hurt you, there is a way to offer forgiveness and yet set protective boundaries. David didn't kill Saul, but he also stayed away from Saul so that Saul couldn't kill him. If you are interested in this, I have included an outline and sample letter of sorts to help you think through how to set boundaries as well as how to address the other person about them.[12]

Mark 11:25 makes this first step of forgiveness most clear: "And, whenever you stand praying, forgive, if you have anything against anyone." Basically, anytime you are praying and think of someone you are angry at, you should forgive them on the spot in your prayers and in your heart. At a minimum this means that you pray and ask God to help you to do that if it currently seems impossible.

Second, we must decide if the sin is small enough to overlook it. Proverbs 19:11 teaches that it is glorious for humans to overlook an offense. Why is it so glorious? Because it is so God like! How often do we sin in a day and forget to specifically apologize to God, and in his great mercy, he just forgives us, and our relationship is not hindered in any way!? We should be like him as much as we can.

So, say your mother was a very practical woman and a little emotionally cold. You have two memories where you tried to talk to her, and she didn't listen perfectly. It hurts you a little. But she has gotten much better. And it is so small in the grand scheme of things. It may be that you should pray and forgive her in your heart and just move on. But this is often not the case.

If you had a dad who was lazy and undisciplined with money, this might have led you to be serious about making and saving money early in life. Imagine you got a job at age fourteen and worked all the way through high school. But your dad would often sneak into your room and take cash. If you confronted him, he laughed and said he was just collecting rent. You had no real recourse. For years you have lived with anger and

---

12. See appendix B for more.

bitterness buried in your heart. It is not realistic to just overlook it. Almost certainly there will need to be some type of confrontation. Often this will not happen face-to-face but in written form or with a third-party mediator. Matthew 18:15 and Luke 17:3 both speak of such a confrontation.

The goal of these confrontations is forgiveness, reconciliation, and freedom. It is never merely just to vent your rage, get something off your chest, or villainize the other person. But for there to be real forgiveness and reconciliation the sin must be clear.

Whether something happened with your spouse last night or with a coach twenty years ago, it is best to pray about forgiving them in your heart. If you think you can overlook it, try to. But if you wake up the next morning and are still bothered by it, then you haven't been able to overlook it. Don't put off the confrontation. It is best to address it if you can't overlook it, even if that needs to be done by phone call.

Third, if you do confront them and they repent for their sin, then you must grant forgiveness. This is the reconciliation that Luke 17:4 speaks of. I can offer forgiveness in my heart like Jesus did on the cross and like Mark 11:25 instructs us to. I should offer it regardless of what the other person does or doesn't do. Remember, when Jesus prayed for his enemies, they were in the middle of torturing and killing him. Yet he offered forgiveness. He had a heart of forgiveness. But forgiveness isn't granted or applied until the other person owns their sin and repents.

Offering forgiveness is a one-way street you can control, in the power of the Holy Spirit. To reconcile, or grant forgiveness, it takes two to tango. It is a two-way street. If there is no repentance, there can be no reconciliation. But this should always be the highest hope, goal, prayer, and dream. But it can't be our ultimate expectation because that is beyond our control and our responsibility.

Fourth, if you confront someone and they refuse to repent, then you are not reconciled. But you must stay with the heart of wanting to forgive, longing to forgive, being ready to forgive, yearning to forgive, and even trying to forgive. "If possible, so far as it depends on you, be at peace with all men" (Rom 12:18). Do all you can to reconcile, but don't carry the burden of their repentance. That is not up to you. You are free if you have offered forgiveness and they refuse to repent. But keep your heart soft so that Satan finds no foothold in you.

Lastly, whether there is reconciliation or not, sometimes there must be consequences. If a father abused a child, the police should be called and that man should go to jail, even if he repents and reconciles with his daughter and becomes a Christian. If an alcoholic mother refuses to quit drinking, you might make a personal boundary that you will not see her, even on Christmas day, if she has been drinking that day. But even within boundaries, there can and should be a heart of mercy, love, and forgiveness. Forgiveness and boundaries are not antithetical. God fully forgave David for his terrible sins. And yet there were terrible consequences for his adultery and murder. His baby died. Second Samuel 12 tells the story. Proverbs 3 and Heb 12 both clearly teach that God disciplines his children.[13]

I've done my best to give a five-step overview of the process. If the process is so biblical and clear, why is it still so often hard, messy, and complicated? Simple does not always mean easy because of all the pain, scars, and hurts of years of sin. We are often very hurt, angry, and ashamed. And we also lack faith. Right after Christ taught on this subject, his disciples said to him, "Increase our faith!" (Luke 17:5). It takes a lot of faith in God's goodness and power to protect you from your enemies if you are going to go and try and reconcile like this. Ephesians 6:16 tells us to take "up the shield of faith with which you will be able to extinguish all the flaming missiles of the evil one."

To practice this process, we must have extraordinarily strong faith to protect us from Satan's schemes and darts. He seeks to shoot lies, doubts, and accusations into our hearts to burn with the fires of rage, fear, and fury. These sins will keep us enslaved to bitterness if we let them. Satan loves to divide believers. He thrives amid human conflict.

John Gil teaches that these temptations are called "flaming" in Eph 6 because "they serve to inflame the mind, and excite to sin."[14] Satan is an expert at bringing up old hurts and helping us nurse them so an anger that had almost died down is rekindled. Have you ever had the experience where in your mind you are having a hypothetical conversation with the person who wronged you? You imagine yourself heatedly telling them exactly what you think of them. Or you can see yourself in a debate with them, proving them wrong, exposing all their sin. It feels so good! Yet it is so dangerous. Often this can be the means of Satan sending a fiery dart into our heart to stoke the fires of sinful anger. I have a friend who is a Presbyterian pastor who believes that when we do this we are conversing with a demon in our mind. The demon is helping this imaginary

---

13. Again, appendix B may be helpful in this regard.
14. Gil, *Exposition of the New Testament*, 111.

conversation to continue to stoke the sinful fear and anger. Whether that is true or not, I do know that Satan will use any means necessary to keep us in sin. And keeping us simmering with low-grade resentment and bitterness is unfortunately not that hard.

John Stott, speaking of Satan says, "He prefers to seduce us into compromise and deceive us into error.... Darts are unsought thoughts of doubt and disobedience."[15] We must daily wake up and remember we are in a war. There is no off day from fighting temptation and indwelling sin.

APPLICATION

We must have faith in God's larger story. What is God seeking to do in and through our lives? Where is there evidence of his grace, even in our painful human stories?

Often when I teach the Bible somewhere, someone will approach me with a question when I'm done. Often the question will be something like this: "I am trying to walk with God and do all I know to be close to him, but I feel so dry spiritually and far from him. What should I do?"

I will start by asking if there is any hidden sin where they are not really repenting and haven't confessed to anyone else. Sometimes they will say yes but usually they say no. Then I will ask them if there is anyone in life they are holding a grudge against or refusing to forgive. Most of the time, their heads will hang and then they will tell me that there is someone.

This is interesting for a couple of reasons. First, when I ask them if there's any hidden or undealt with sin, they are quick to say no. They don't think of withholding forgiveness as sin. But so often that is the root cause of someone feeling far from God even as they try and seek him daily in prayer and the word and Christian fellowship, etc.

Matthew 6:12–15 shows us how important our forgiving of others is. It's part of the Lord's Prayer. "And forgive us our debts, as we also have forgiven our debtors" (Matt 6:12). Most of us have prayed for this literally a thousand times, but have we really thought out the implications? What does it mean?

Alone and out of context it seems to teach a works-based salvation. If I forgive others, then God will forgive me. But the rest of the Bible testifies against that. We must interpret Scripture in light of Scripture. First John 4:19 is one clear example: "We love, because He first loved us."

---

15. Stott, *Ephesians*, 265, 281.

And this is a prayer for those who are saved. Jesus is teaching his disciples to pray, and the prayer starts with "Our Father" (Matt 6:9). So then, what does Matt 6:12 mean? Here is my best understanding. Christians have God's cosmic legal forgiveness in the courtroom of the universe, for all past, present, and future sins, the moment they trust in Christ the first time. But they will not always experience a sense of that forgiveness. To experience that forgiveness, we must also be practicing it.

It is as if God says, "If you refuse to practice this forgiveness with others, I won't let you feel it from me, although you still have it." Imagine you decided you didn't like the feeling of air going out of your throat, so you decided to constrict your throat so no more air would ever leave your windpipe. This is an unwise decision for multiple reasons. But the worst is that, if your windpipe is totally closed off from air leaving your body, then air cannot enter either. Without oxygen you die.

In a similar fashion if we refuse to practice God's marvelous forgiveness to those who have wronged us, we will notice that our experience of God's forgiveness will lessen. Partially, the Holy Spirit is grieved when we nurse our anger in this way. He withdraws a sense of his smile and presence (see Eph 4:26–30).

Have you ever hurt your spouse, friend, child, or parent? Even if this is the person that loves you most on planet earth, they may need space from you. If you say something terribly painful to your best friend, it may make sense that they hang their head in sadness and pain and go to their room and shut the door and ask to be alone for a while. They aren't leaving you or divorcing you. They do need space and time to heal. And in a similar fashion, when a genuine Christian grieves the Holy Spirit, he will never leave you nor forsake you, but he may withdraw a sense of his gracious presence at times.

John MacArthur teaches that forgiveness is the most divine thing we can do. I agree. I would add that holding a grudge and refusing to forgive may be the most satanic thing we can do. We must take this sin seriously.

Why is Satan fighting so hard even though he knows he is defeated? He's angry, bitter, and just can't let it go. Is there anywhere in life where you are acting like him? If so, repent quickly!

Why do we have such a tough time with this? Because the gospel in our lives is often like a black and white TV with no sound. We can see the pictures and follow the story, but it doesn't interest us much. It doesn't impact us as it should.

But the past pain and hurt in our own lives and stories is like one of those 4DX experiences where you can see, feel, hear, smell, and taste the reality of what happened from all directions. It is overwhelming to your senses. Oftentimes our spiritual senses are overwhelmed with past hurt and trauma.

I know a college student who wasn't the smartest guy in the world. He wanted to know what it would be like to be sprayed by a skunk. Like I said, he was not the smartest. He found a skunk. He chased it. He threw things at it. It sprayed him. There's video evidence. The spray hit him right in the face. He later said that it smelled so bad and horrid that his ability to smell shut down. His body was protecting him from suffering.

Some of us have suffered so terribly in our lives that our spiritual senses have shut down. We have forgotten what it is like to feel safe, loved, and protected. It's too dangerous to let our guards down. So, we keep them up, we hold the grudge, and we stay dead inside. We may be dead to the past pain, but when we deaden our emotions in one area or direction, all our emotions tend to deaden together. So, even our good emotions and affections that should be experiencing God's goodness and love are deadened as well.

We may pay lip service to the gospel, but we pay life service to the pain, the hurts, the bitterness. Hebrews 12:14–15 teaches that bitterness is like a root. It is often underground and unseen. But it is alive. It's deadly. And it's growing. And it will bear a poisonous, life-killing fruit.

Faith is seeing God's victory over the sin, the lies, and the bad circumstance of life, including all the pain and hurt that flow from them. Faith is truly believing and feeling that God's word about you is truer than what the circumstances may seem to say about you. People's sins against us are the smaller stories. Satan is trying to play your past sin and hurt story on HD with surround sound constantly in your mind. We must learn to turn the volume down on his story and turn the volume up on God's truer and larger story.

Imagine a man who is engaged to a woman he is madly in love with. But that woman cheats on him, breaks his heart, and seemingly ruins his life. The engagement is broken, and he feels like he will never recover. He goes to counseling. His counselor happens to be a godly woman who is single. Through the counseling process, they fall in love; they get married. (I'm not sure that's technically ethical for counselors, but just go with it for now for the sake of illustration!)

Not only that, but the man is amazed at how much the counseling helped him; he quits his job and becomes a full-time counselor. Now he is much more fulfilled in his career, and his marriage is better than he could have ever even imagined when he was engaged to the first woman. One day he runs into the woman who broke his heart. It should be much easier to fully forgive her now because so much good came out of the hurt she caused.

The power of the pain the cheater caused the man should fade into the background because of all the good that later came. The good news of the story in some sense cancels out and overwhelms all the scars of the past. The cheater still sinned. The cheater should still be confronted and repent. And yet it ought to be so much easier to extend forgiveness to someone when you see how it ended for your betterment.

If you have pain in your life that still overwhelms and controls you, there is hope. Spend some time this week journaling and meditating on Rom 8:28. Specifically, try to find any and every good thing that God has done in your life that has roots in the trauma you experienced. Do not rush this process. Maybe make it part of your daily time alone with the Lord for a while. But please do not procrastinate on this process either. Take steps to get your heart and mind off the small story of sin and hurt and onto the larger story of salvation and hope.

CONCLUSION

Who has hurt you in life? Who has been used by Satan to lie to you? Who might you still need to forgive?

That sweet story above I made up may sound too saccharine for you. It may remind you of a bad Hallmark movie that played in the middle of a workday. Well, here is a true story from the book of Genesis.

There was a teenage boy named Jo. He lived in a mixed family. His dad had been married multiple times. He had ten older brothers from different moms who seemed to really hate him.

One day they ambushed him, ganged up on him, and beat him. They seriously discussed killing him. But then they decided on perhaps a worst fate. They literally found a way to sell their brother into slavery. They ignored his cries for help.

Once in slavery things started to look up for him in some sense. He was bought by a wealthy man who allowed him to be more of a household manager. He got to work inside and manage much of the man's business and finances, etc. But then his owner's wife took a liking to him. She tried to seduce him. But he stood strong and resisted. The scorned woman decided to falsely accuse him of rape. He was thrown into prison.

In prison he tried to help others. Others promised to help him, but they didn't. They forgot him. It would be easy to see how Satan would lie to him and say, "You are unloved. You are uncared for. You are not special. No one really cares for you. No one remembers you. Your own brothers tried to kill you. You were sold into slavery. Your own dad never even came looking for you. Even when you do right, you're not rewarded in the long run. Even God doesn't love you or care or pay attention to your suffering!"

But one day he was released from prison and literally became the prime minister of the most powerful nation on planet earth. A famine was coming. He was put in charge of planning to survive. He led the nation to save a lot of grain that they could later sell to starving people.

One day his brothers came to buy grain from him, not knowing who he was. He confronted them and tested them. They seemed repentant. All the while he had a forgiving heart. He wanted to forgive them. He was hoping to reconcile.

When he saw they were genuinely repentant, he revealed his identity, forgave them, and reconciled. He never brushed over their sin or said it wasn't a big deal. No, he called it evil, as it was. But he saw how God had done something beautiful out of their sin and so he forgave them.

Joseph later said, "You meant evil against me, but God meant it for good" (Gen 50:20). God plans all things that happen to us. He orchestrates it all. This may seem to make things worse at first, knowing God is behind our worst pain in some sense. But it makes things better because if God is behind it all then he can control, manage, and fix it all.

Joseph knew his brothers were still responsible for their sin and needed to show changed lives of repentance before they could be trusted again. But he also saw the beauty and power of God's plan. God used this evil to accomplish great good. God was doing something much bigger than allowing brothers to hurt a younger sibling. God was putting Joseph in a place of power and blessing so that he could become a blessing to so many others!

Joseph had real, experiential faith in the goodness, power, and wisdom of God over all things, including the pain of his life. Even the evil sin of his brothers that hurt him so badly was part of God's pristine and perfect plan. Believing this freed Joseph from being bitter and angry and thus controlled by Satan. He had faith in the larger story of what God was doing all those years behind the scenes.

My wife grew up in a poor, broken, non-Christian home with much pain and sadness. She spent years working through broken relationships with her mom and dad, moving to a place where she could genuinely forgive them. She took the hard and courageous step of both confronting them and offering forgiveness. Her dad never really repented. There was no reconciliation. But she tried. Her mom did repent, and they did reconcile. But because of my wife's faithfulness in both relationships, she was really freed from anger, hurt, and bitterness.

One day, out of the blue, she said to me, "I'm glad it happened. I'm thankful now for the way I grew up. I see now how God has used it for the good in my life in so many ways. Mainly I see how he has enabled me to minister to so many others with similar stories."

This often seems to be God's pattern. He ordains pain and hardship in our lives to grow and mature us. But then the place of our deepest hurt and wound becomes the place of strength where we can help and minister to so many others if we trust him. God comforts us in affliction so we can turn and use that God-given comfort to minister to others in similar afflictions (2 Cor 1:3–7). Forgiving those who have hurt us is one of the biggest and clearest steps of trusting his word over our circumstances.

I have another friend who grew up with a lying, abusive, hypocritical dad. I am not sure he's ever fully forgiven his dad. And this man is an elder in a great church with great theology. But as we talked about his past and his relationship with his dad, he said to me one day, "I finally know what my problem is. I don't really believe Romans 8:28 is true. I don't really believe God works all for my good." Unfortunately, I think this is where many Christians live—even Christians that have Rom 8:28 memorized or written on a note and stuck on to their bathroom mirror.

You may have much pain in your life that is ongoing. You may not have seen Rom 8:28 flesh out in your life yet. You may not see the arc of the circle beginning to bend back away from burden and towards blessings yet. This can make it harder to forgive, especially when your enemies continue to sin against you.

But, if you are in Christ, you should be able to taste and see the beauty of Rom 8:28 so clearly and deeply, even if your life is still filled with the pain. The greatest example of God working all for the good of his people is the cross. The end of all history has been written. In some sense, it's already happened.

Jesus was the truer and greater Joseph. He came to his own people, his brothers, but they hated him. They were jealous of him (John 11:48 shows this). They mocked him, beat him, imprisoned him, and then they gave him up to another nation to kill him.

Joseph had no choice but to suffer. He could only choose how he would respond. This is true of us as well. The Lord Jesus did have a choice and could have quit and tapped out at any point. Yet, he stayed. He trusted and obeyed.

Jesus became a man and lived a sinless life for sinners like you and me. He suffered and died under the wrath of God for the sins of his people. Out of his great love and mercy towards us, he looked at the wrath of his Father bearing down on us and willingly took it in our stead. He did this so that he could forgive us and help us forgive others!

The gospel is the truer and greater story that you and I must meditate on daily. For many of us our surrounding circumstances speak to us powerfully. They are like a surround-sound, 4DX theater experience that has sounds, shaking, smells, and wind blowing through our hair to try and convince us that we have truly been transported to another land. Satan uses circumstances to convince us we have been transported away from the Father's love.

Far too many of us experience God's truth like a dim radio signal barely getting through. We must flip these two metaphors. We must learn to minimize the power that our circumstances have in us. We must turn up the volume on the truth of God's word so that it comes into our lives daily, loud, clear, and transforming.

God uses pain for our good. He accomplishes his greatest victories through suffering. He proved it on the cross. Trust him. Love and forgive your enemies. Be free from sin, from Satan, and from his lies!

If you've ever walked through a haunted house, it can feel terrifying in the moment, but you know it's not real. So, you fight to stay calm even as you hear a chain saw or someone screaming. In a similar way, life is scary. And it often hurts. Life is real and I'm not trying to minimize that. I am saying the gospel is more real. It is more enduring. This life will soon be over with all its pain. "He shall wipe away every tear from their eyes; and there shall no longer be any death; there shall no longer be any mourning, or crying, or pain (Rev 21:4). The gospel story is more powerful and pertinent.

If you are in Christ, you have seen the end of your story by faith. The life, death, and resurrection of Christ brought the end of history into the middle of history so we can know how it all ends. God's people win big! Trust God's plan even when life seems to scream something different at you. Satan may say the opposite of what God says. He may say it in very powerful and convincing ways at times. But he is wrong. God is right. Rest in the reality of God's greater story for you!

Chapter 10

Fight for Faith

Matthew 14; Luke 5, 22; Galatians 2; 1 Peter 5

The goal of this book has been to see and slay Satan's schemes. This chapter aims to help you identify your own lies and to develop strategies to fight them. We first must identify the beginnings of sin in our lives and hopefully stop it before it begins to gain more traction in our lives. This is much harder than we might imagine. We have three enemies: sinful world culture, indwelling sin, and the devil. Indwelling sin is usually baked into us, rooted deeply in us much more than we understand.

We've spent much of the book looking at how Satan lies to us. There are at least four main categories of lies. We see them clearly in Adam and Eve, as well as others.

The first lie is "God is not good enough." The insinuation is that God is trying to oppress you and hold you back. He is not giving you the best stuff in life you want, deserve, or feel that you need.

The second is "You're not good enough." You lack something. You are fundamentally broken. There is no hope for you in God and his ways. The only chance you have is to fix yourself. Pull yourself up by your bootstraps.

The third is "Life's not good enough." You need forbidden fruit to make life work for you. If you really want to be happy, you will have to break some of God's rules. Do whatever it takes to dull, numb, and mute the pain and pressure of life, even if it requires sinning a little.

The fourth is "the gospel's not good enough." You must cover yourself. You must lie. You must hide. You must blame shift, rationalize, and explain away your guilt. Save yourself! Develop some form of fig-leaf righteousness to make yourself look better to a watching world.

In the previous chapter we looked at the idea of forgiving others. This can be an extension of the fourth lie. The gospel is not good enough to protect me in my human relationships so I must protect myself by holding onto to hate and anger. Or if the fourth lie is "the gospel isn't good enough for you," by extension the fifth lie is "the gospel isn't good enough for others either."[1]

In this chapter we are going to look at how the first four of these lies played out in the life of one man. We want to learn how to identify these four lies as they come up in our lives so that we can fight and kill them. Looking at examples like this in others' lives helps us do that.

GOD IS NOT GOOD ENOUGH

Luke 5:4–11 details for us Peter's official call to become a full-time follower of Christ, one of his apprentices. He would now be a minister in training. He's being prepared to be an apostle and the leader of the early church.

Peter has been fishing all night. He has caught nothing. Jesus tells him to fish a little more. Peter responds that he doubts it will do much good, but he is willing to give it a try.

There may have been some pride in Peter's response. There may have been a sense of him thinking, "Jesus, you're a great teacher and I'm a great fisherman. You stick to teaching and let me handle fishing. But to humor you and show you you're wrong, I'll put back out to sea for a bit."

We don't know for sure. Let's give Peter the benefit of the doubt. Let's say he has a great attitude and is quickly willing to do exactly what Jesus asks.

He obeys and they quickly catch so many fish that his boat almost sinks with the blessing of God! Now, you would expect his response to be happy and joyful. You would expect delight and celebration and praise! But he didn't dance for joy.

He begs Jesus to leave. He is convicted of his sinfulness. He is in the presence of Jesus and realizes how different they are, at least to some degree, and he is humbled. He is amazed at the miracle. It seems his faith is growing. He is realizing more and more that Jesus is more than a mere man.

---

1. Appendix C provides an overview summary of these five lies.

I used to teach this passage as a good example of the fear of the Lord. But the more I studied and meditated, the more I realized that is not what this is. Want to know why?

Jesus tells Peter to stop being afraid. His response was, "Do not fear" (Luke 5:10). Jesus wouldn't have rebuked Peter for having proper fear of God. This was sinful fear.

Why was Peter fearful in this passage? He saw the power of Christ and maybe his wisdom. But he did not really see his goodness. He did not understand his love.

He saw some of the glory of Jesus and thought of his own sinfulness and despaired and feared. He didn't rightly see the mercy and grace of Christ. That's why Christ told him to quit fearing and to rise and follow him.

God is a God who delights to pardon his people. Christ came to make that clear. Peter didn't see that at first. But his faith was weak and small. Yet, it was growing.

YOU ARE NOT GOOD ENOUGH

In Matt 14:24–31 we again find Peter in a boat talking to Jesus. The disciples are in a boat together, on the sea, experiencing rough weather. Jesus comes walking to them on the waves, in the storm.

The disciples see him, assume he is a ghost, and are afraid. They should have known better. They should have known Jesus was near and loved them and would protect them. But they didn't think about that truth at that moment and thus gave into their fears.

Again, in Matt 14:27, Jesus says, "Do not be afraid." Both times it is the word of Christ that frees people from their sinful fear. Meditate on this truth!

Peter responds well. He is not being rash. He doesn't just jump into the stormy waters. Rather, he waits for the word of Christ. "Lord, if it is You, command me to come to You on the water" (Matt 14:28).

He gets Christ's command to come. He steps out of the boat and onto the water. He literally walks on water. He focuses on Christ and walks towards him. He is living a miracle while his eyes are locked onto Christ. But this doesn't last.

His faith weakens and his fear grows. He looks at the waves. He gets his eyes off Christ and onto other circumstances and begins to sink. Fear returns.

Still, he prays. He cries out for mercy and help. Christ comes near. He grabs his hand. He lifts him up. He saves him. Yet, he also gently rebukes him.

In v. 31, Jesus asks, "O you of little faith, why did you doubt." He doesn't accuse him of having no faith. He just has small faith, weak faith.

Satan lies to us about who God is. "Maybe he won't help you or save you." He also lies to us about ourselves. "You are too far gone. There is no hope for you. You are eternally condemned!" When we listen to one or both lies, we will begin to sink. We will begin to doubt God's love, goodness, kindness, and sufficiency for us in all things.

Fear and doubt are two different ways to describe the same thing. At the deepest root, all sin starts with fear and doubt. Even if on the surface this does not seem to be the case, trace the root down deep. At the bottom level you will find some form of fear and doubt.

Imagine someone who sinfully indulges in their appetites. Overeating, over sleeping, getting drunk, watching porn, and more doesn't really seem like a type of fear at all. Have you heard of FOMO, the fear of missing out? If I fear I won't get the best things in life from living God's ways, this will drive me into all types of indulgences. I will be willing to break many rules, cross many lines, and sin many sins if that's what it takes to get the pleasure, provision, or protection I feel I need.

If I am too focused on my feelings, emotions, desires, and circumstances, I will sin. I must be more focused on Christ than the other realities around me. This takes a life time of practice to change.

R. T. France explains the doubt Peter experienced as he began to sink. It "denotes not so much a theological uncertainty or unbelief as a practical hesitation, wavering, being in two minds[,] . . . not so much lack of intellectual conviction as the conflict between the evidence of his senses and the invitation of Jesus."[2] This sounds like us does it not? We may say we believe in Jesus so much we are ready and willing to die for him. But in the day-to-day temptations of life, we waver. We hesitate. We question. We doubt. We get overwhelmed. We mediate more on the "evidence of senses" than on the "invitation of Jesus." Where is Jesus calling you to trust him and obey him? Where is he inviting you to experience more of him? Are you holding back in fear?

When we have times like this, of wavering and doubt, it isn't that our theological convictions go out the window for good. Rather, we

---

2. France, *Matthew*, 570–71.

experience the tension in the difference between what we say we believe and what we have truly experienced. Imagine that a friend asks for advice on how to handle a rebellious child struggling with drunkenness. You might be able to give a brilliant, accurate, helpful answer about speaking the truth calmly and in love. Later that same night if one of your own teenagers stumbles in drunk, you might not follow your own advice. You might feel so much anger and shame in that moment that you blow up and scream. It's not that you did not know the right thing to do. But when push came to shove, you didn't fully trust in the advice you had paid lip service to earlier. None of our lives are as good as the theology we claim to believe.

D. A. Carson says that Jesus's "rhetorical question . . . helps both Peter and the reader recognize that doubts and fears disappear before a strict inquiry into their cause."[3] We must learn to catch ourselves in the moment of doubt and fear and ask ourselves, "Why am I doubting? What am I afraid of?" This will help us clarify the lie that Satan may be trying to convince us of in that moment. If we learn to do this, we will often be able to catch and repent of sin before it even begins to blossom in our lives.

LIFE IS NOT GOOD ENOUGH

In Luke 22 Jesus warns Peter that Satan is personally coming after him. Put yourself in Peter's shoes for a moment. The Lord of the universe tells you that Satan is coming after you today. How might you respond? You would think there would be high levels of dependence, sobriety, and humility. But that's not how Peter responded.

Jesus goes on to tell him more. He essentially says, "Peter, you are going to fall into sin tonight. But I am praying for you. You won't utterly fail and fall away for good. You will rise again. You will be restored. You will lead again." In one sense this is terrifying, but it is also very encouraging. We may wonder why Peter didn't ask, "Jesus, why didn't you just tell Satan no?! Don't let him sift me like wheat!"

This should be sobering for us, as much as for Peter, in some ways. We have two clear examples in the Bible where Satan asks permission to tempt someone, Job and Peter. The comforting reality is to know Satan is on a leash and can't touch us unless God says OK. The terrifying thing is that both times God essentially said, "Go for it." He put some minor limits on Job's trials. But not many.

3. Carson, *Matthew*, 344.

This seems to be the normal pattern of the universe. Satan asks to tempt God's people. God says yes within some incredibly broad parameters. Satan starts the trial. We may respond well in the beginning, but in the short run we usually stumble and fall somewhere along the way. The more we can understand about these patterns of temptation, the better we will be able to stand next time they come.

Sometimes when Satan is lying to us, we give into doubt and fear and just crumble. That's what we saw Peter do in the first two examples in this chapter. The same thing can happen to us. Maybe you have a clear opportunity to share the gospel with a friend, but in the moment evil thoughts start to come to mind. "What am I doing? I am not smart enough to answer all his questions. My life is a mess. I have no right to speak of Christ. I am a hypocrite. This friend doesn't trust or respect me. I'm a failure!" As the thoughts build, we can give into the lies and give up before we ever start. But that's not always how we respond to Satan's attacks.

Other times we try and compensate. We try to push back and fight lies in our own strength. Pride and overconfidence win the day. This is what Peter did on this fateful night. His attitude was, "I've got this. Nothing to worry about Lord. You can count on me through thick and thin. I'm with you to the end. These other idiots may abandon you. Sure, I can see them falling. But me? Never! I can manage this situation and make things better. Trust me!"

Peter didn't listen to a personalized warning straight from the mouth of Christ. And this will be when he falls in the worst way. We must take God's word so seriously. Pride at some level says, "I don't like God's plan for my life. I'll go a different way. I'll ignore God's word." That's what Peter did that night. Jesus told him he would fall. In his pride, he said, "There's no way that's true. Sorry, Jesus, you're wrong again. I will not betray you!" This is like the pride he had in Matt 16 when he pulled Jesus aside to rebuke him for all that negative self-talk about having to die on the cross.

When the soldiers come into the garden Peter first pulls out his sword and tries to fight. He was true to his word. He wasn't bluffing that he wanted to stick with Christ. His spirit was willing. His flesh was weak.

Jesus tells him to put the sword away. At that point Peter sees Jesus arrested and is probably shocked and turns to run. But he changes his mind. You can see the second half of Rom 7 playing out in Peter's life that night. He wants to follow Jesus but struggles to do it. He runs away—the very thing he said he would never do. But he battles. He catches himself and turns back to follow again, though at a distance. Isn't this what we often do? We follow Christ from afar, wavering between fear and faith?

A woman in the courtyard identifies Peter. He denies knowing Jesus. Then he denies knowing him again. The fear seems to be winning over his faith. Then the fateful third time he denies knowing his Savior, much less loving him and being willing to die for him.

Just at this moment, Jesus looks at Peter and Peter breaks. He runs away but he weeps. There is true remorse, true grief over sin. It is a sin to give into fear and doubt. It is also a sin to respond with an arrogant, "no problem, I've got this" attitude. Which do you struggle with more?

Calvin gives a helpful reminder. The devil "pops in as soon as he finds a breach, just waiting for the door to be opened. Indeed, he knows how to enter without being invited, just asking for a little crack. This is a warning to us that when we have made a good resolution, we must do all we can to keep from changing it, our of fear of giving the devil an opening. Although we are on our guard, he will still find enough leeway."[4] If Satan could influence Peter so much while Peter was in the presence of Christ physically, certainly he is able to influence us as well.

GOSPEL IS NOT GOOD ENOUGH

Peter was the first one to preach to the gentiles in Acts 10. In Acts 11:1–3 circumcised believers took issue with him when he got back to Jerusalem. He had to explain himself. He did explain himself and did so well that he convinced his detractors.

But there was still a lot of tension in the new church between Jews and gentiles. One of the main issues was whether they should eat together. The Old Testament ceremonial law had taught that Jews could not eat certain foods. It never said that Jews could not eat with gentiles. But for various reasons many devout Jews refused to eat with gentiles. Many probably saw it as a way to keep ritual purity but also to make sure they obeyed the Mosaic law and avoided even accidentally eating some of the forbidden foods.

When Jesus came, he ended the ceremonial law and thus declared all foods clean (Mark 7:19). He even personally made this clear to Peter in a vision in Acts 10. So, Peter knew and understood this reality very well.

---

4. Calvin, *Sermons*, 624.

Galatians 2:12–14 tells a story of Peter visiting Antioch. This church had many gentile converts. Peter felt very free in Christ and often ate with them.

But then a group of Jewish men came to Antioch from Jerusalem. At minimum they were professing believers. They may have been immature believers. They were seemingly sent by James, the brother of Jesus, who was now serving as the head pastor of the megachurch in Jerusalem. The church in Jerusalem was primarily made up of Jewish converts.

Many of these Jews from Jerusalem would have leaned towards the legalistic side. Many probably still obeyed the ceremonial law as well as stuck to ancient customs from Judaism that weren't necessarily written down. They would not have been comfortable eating with gentile converts.

Now Peter is getting fearful again. He was the apostle to the Jews. In some sense, he should have been the most confident man in the room. But he doesn't want his name tarnished back in Jerusalem. He doesn't want word getting out among the megachurch and his reputation and popularity with Jewish believers to be lessened. So, he makes a fateful decision.

Peter slowly stopped eating with the gentiles. We don't know exactly how this went down, but it seems he gradually sat at the same table with them less and less. It was like a strategic retreat, a calculated withdrawal. In his fear, he is willing to hurt other believers to protect his pride.

At some level he wanted to keep his Jewish reputation untarnished. He wanted his record to be clean. In a functional way, he wanted his personal righteousness to remain intact. He was attempting to rest on his own righteous record.

If you think I'm going too far, look at how the apostle Paul responds. He happened to be in town at the same time and saw what was going down. Paul is wise and quickly deduces the sin. Maybe no one else fully understood what Peter was doing. Paul did.

Paul doesn't attack Peter about an eating issue or the ceremonial law. He doesn't bring up racial or cultural biases. He doesn't talk about being nice and friendly. Rather, he gets to the heart of the matter. It is a gospel issue.

Galatians 2:14 records Paul telling Peter that his life doesn't line up with the gospel. If the gospel was Peter's only hope, boast, confidence, and perfect righteousness, Peter wouldn't be sinfully worried about his reputation. If Christ is my reputation, who cares what the Jewish Christians think about me. I am free (see 1 Cor 4:1–5 for more on this).

This event happened at least fourteen years after the resurrection of Christ. The Holy Spirit has been given. Peter has been the leader of the church for over a decade. And yet he, like us, still struggles with old sin patterns. He struggled with fear and doubt as the deepest root sin, just as we do. Then he struggled with his own attempts to cover up his sin with more sin in the form of pride and boasting in himself and his abilities and his own righteousness. He coveted a great reputation with Jewish Christians.

Luther says, "Peter knew the article of justification better than we do, and yet how easily he gave great occasion of offense."[5] If he fell so quickly and easily from gospel living, how much quicker and easier might you and I fall? We must be sober minded and set our minds daily on gospel truth.

Richard Lovelace is helpful on these issues as well.

> Men who are not secure in Christ cast about for spiritual life preservers with which to support their confidence, and in their frantic search they not only cling to the shreds of ability and righteousness they find in themselves, but they fix upon race, their membership in a party, their familiar social and ecclesiastical patterns, and their culture as a means of self-recommendation. The culture is put on as though it were armor against self-doubt, but it becomes a mental straitjacket which cleaves to the flesh and can never be removed except through comprehensive faith in the saving work of Christ.[6]

Peter felt insecure. He was willing to boast in his Jewish or cultural purity to make himself feel better about himself and to look better to the Jews from Jerusalem. How about you? Where do you most often feel insecure? In those desperate moments, what do you cling to? Do you boast about your accomplishments, your intellect, your good looks, your money, or your athletic ability? Maybe like Peter you boast about your spiritual achievements or heritage. You may not do it out loud but only silently to yourself in your heart and mind to make yourself feel more secure. The fact is in those moments we must boast and hope more fully and deeply in the finished work of Christ for us that secures us not only in this life but also in the life to come.

---

5. Luther, *Galatians*, 83.
6. Lovelace, *Dynamics*, 198, 212.

APPLICATION

I'm highlighting how Peter failed, not to make us hopeless but to make us more sober about the fight ahead. I know I often hear one great sermon and think, "I'll never sin in that same way again. It's clear now. I know what to do!" It may be three weeks or three months later, but the old struggle will raise its head again. Perhaps I've had a great worship experience where I feel in the depths of being free from Satan's lies and accusations. "By grace I'll never give into those thought patterns again," I may declare. But the battle will rage on.

How about you? Have you ever developed what felt like the perfect accountability plan or committed to a new Scripture memory regiment or planned regular days of fasting and prayer and thought, "That's it! This old sin pattern will now be gone in my life!?" We desperately want to be fixed and healed. We want obedience to come nice and easy. But we forget we are in a war and Satan hasn't laid down yet. Nor has indwelling sin. This is a fight to death. We will live in the second half of Rom 7 until we see Jesus, face-to-face.

Peter saw the resurrected Christ. Peter experienced Pentecost. Yet he fell again. This is not to discourage you. It is to wake us up.

Jesus was literally right in front of Peter physically performing a miracle, walking on the water. Peter was experiencing a miracle. He too was walking on the waves. Even in that supernatural moment, doubt and lies came and he sank. He lost his focus on Christ. How much more likely are we to do the same when we can't see, touch, and hear Christ physically?

If Peter heard the personal warning of Christ verbally and missed it, how much more danger is there for us? We must fight through the word and prayer to always stay fixed on Christ's word. It is not natural or easy. But when we do, it is a game changer.

Luther said, "There is nothing better than to have the Word of God before your eyes, and therein to seek the comfort of the Spirit. . . . I have suffered many and various passions, and the same also very vehement and great. But as soon as I have laid hold of any place of Scripture, and stayed myself upon it as upon my chief anchor-hold, immediately temptations vanished away; without the Word it would have been impossible to overcome them."[7] Scripture meditation personally applied to specific lies and temptations is such a key in this fight.

---

7. Luther, *Galatians*, 369.

We must stay ready daily for the fight. Our spirit is willing like Peter's. Our flesh is weak as well. We must watch and pray that we won't be overcome with temptation (Luke 22:40). Keller reminds us, "It is under stress, in real experiences, that the true nature of our hearts is revealed."[8] It's easy to walk with God first thing in the morning when all is calm, and we are in our favorite chair with Bible and coffee in hand. Or if we are lying on the beach on vacation with our best friend with perfect weather, it may feel natural to obey the Lord in that moment. But when the pressure of life hits the fan in our hearts, we will see what is really operating in the subterranean basement of our soul. And yet, even after the fight, when we are at rest for a moment, temptation can sneak in. Noah had made it through the flood when he decided to get drunk (Gen 9:20–21). We are never fully safe and fully free of the fight until we are at home with Christ in the next life.

"We must have multiple exposures both to our need for God's grace—which usually come through experiences of disappointment and failure—and to the gospel message. To get God's love and Christ's grace down deep into the motivational principles of our hearts, to the foundational layer of our identities, is a process, and often a slow one."[9] What really drives you? What is the deepest desire of your heart? The more you know yourself, your fears, pride, and drives, the more you can begin to fight and kill sin.

Many years later Peter wrote the letter we now call 1 Peter. In the last chapter he addresses two problems simultaneously. The first, it seems, is that some of the older elders weren't great shepherds of the church. Either they didn't enjoy the task or some may have been motivated to do it only for the pay they received. They were being harsh and lording it over others unkindly.

Secondly, younger people in the church weren't always submitting well to these leaders. This is understandable but not excusable. How will Peter address it?

First, he reminds them all that God is good enough. God has saved us. He plans to take all his people to heaven and give us each a crown. So, older elders, if you have some pride in your reputation or status, lay it down. Don't boast about that. You don't need that. Don't fight for that. God will give you a reputation in heaven better than you can imagine.

---

8. Keller, *Counterfeit Gods*, 144.
9. Keller, *Prodigal Prophet*, 219.

God will vindicate you in this life or the next if your reputation is wrongly tarnished here.

If I believe the lie that God is not good enough, I'll be tempted to find enough good stuff in my life and in my ways of doing life to try and satisfy myself. It will never work. But if I don't believe God can or will ultimately satisfy me, I'll be on a never-ending search here on planet earth that will leave me more and more miserable and unfulfilled.

Next, he addresses the younger people in the church. If you are young among God's people and feel you lack something, don't sinfully assert yourself. Don't sinfully take matters into your own hands to get your way or grab more influence. Don't try so hard to establish and secure your reputation.

Be humble. God will exalt you in the right way, in the right time. It all goes back to living by faith in God's goodness. Don't live by fear. God may exalt you in this life or the next or both. Trust him. Await his wisdom, timing, and ways. Rest.

If you are tempted to worry about your reputation, influence, position, title, future, or whatever, that is very understandable. Life on planet earth is a roller coaster ride happening during an earthquake. Nothing ever feels too secure. But God would tell us all: "Don't worry about it! I've got it under control." We must not fear or doubt. We must not believe the lie that God is not going to give us the best life for us. But we must trust him deeply and fully. Because the perfect life he has planned for his people often won't feel that way to them in the moment. Trust his sovereign and eternal shrewdness.

Sometimes God's best for us in the moment will feel like a beating. It may be an actual beating! Remember the story of Joseph from the end of the last chapter? Part of God's perfect, best plan for Joseph was that his ten older brothers beat him up and throw him in a pit. That seems miserable. But it was God's unique way to begin to move Joseph to be ready to be the prime minister of Egypt. Trust God's heart for you when it's hard to trust the actions of his hand delivered to you through providence.

Trust God. Bring your fears, worries, and doubts to him in prayer. Throw your burdens and cares off your back. Throw them onto him. Leave them there. Let him handle them.

God cares for you. The main and deepest lie Satan ever told is "God doesn't really care for you." The disciples felt it in the boat in the storm. "Teacher, do you not care that we are perishing?" (Mark 4:38). Martha felt it in her home as she compared herself to Mary. "Lord, do you not care that my sister has left me to do all the serving alone?" (Luke 10:40). They saw circumstances in their lives that convinced them God didn't care even though he was physically present with them.

We do not have God's physical presence. Circumstances scream at us, "God does not care for you!" Once we give into this lie, sin has begun. It will grow and multiply until we repent of our false belief.

Satan is real. He is alive. He is stalking God's people. We will suffer. But please do not give into the lie that we must save ourselves. We cannot!

The life of faith is a waiting game. It is not easy. It is a fight to death, literally. We must resist Satan and his lies. Our faith must be alive, vivid, burning, brimming over!

Christ is going to save us completely. If you are in Christ, he has already justified you. He is sanctifying you. He will perfect and glorify you one day very soon. Rest in his finished work.

God is committed to growing us up in Christ. He will take us home. He will establish us. He will secure us.

Don't live by arrogance like you can handle life on your own. Don't live by fear or anxiety, like no one will handle it for you or help you. Live by appropriating the faith that Christ has handled it and will continue to handle you in love and care.

CONCLUSION

As we have seen before Satan pursued Christ with lies as well. Christ provides the perfect model of how to fight lies but also provides much more! Christ lived and died perfectly to be so much more than a model. He is our substitute and Savior!

Christ gave up his experience of the Father's goodness on the cross so that we can have it by faith. Christ gave up his good life that we might have it by faith. Christ suffered willingly. He did not save himself so that he might save all his people.

Quit trying to save yourself. Quit trying to save your life. Be willing to lose your life for Christ's sake. Quit trying to make your life work for you apart from Christ.

Surrender to him afresh. Trust him. Obey him. Wait patiently and humbly for all the good he has in store for you. Be confident. Boast in the finished work of Christ on your behalf!

Chapter 11

Faith vs. Fear

Genesis 25, 27

We have looked at the four main roots of sin in this book. We doubt God's goodness. This lack of faith is fear. We then become proud and think if God won't provide for me, then I'll just provide for myself. We then begin to covet something in life. We find something we believe can give us satisfaction, security, and significance. We feel we must have that thing at all costs. Without it we die. As we follow these sinful pursuits, we begin to feel shame and guilt. We seek to cover our own sin rather than run to Christ. This is sinful self-protection.

In the last chapter we looked at how these lies played out in the life of Peter. In this chapter we will examine the life of Jacob. We will see similar patterns emerge.

DOUBT FROM LACK OF DAD'S LOVE

Genesis 25:21–28 tells us the story of Jacob's conception, birth, and childhood. His father Isaac was the head of the covenant family in Genesis. This was essentially the Old Testament church. He married and then prays for twenty years for his barren wife to have a child. He must have really wanted kids. She finally conceives twins.

Before the twins were born, God said that the younger one would lead the family after Isaac was gone. Tradition said that the oldest male would gain most of the inheritance and keep the family name and wealth strong. But God said it would be the reverse for this family. "The older shall serve the younger" (Gen 25:23).

The twins were born—Esau, the oldest, and Jacob, the younger. They were different from the start. Esau grows up to be a hairy outdoorsman. He is the quintessential man's man who loved to hunt.

Jacob seems to be quieter, tame in ways, more contemplative. He seems to be more of a mama's boy. The story is not saying one personality is better than the other. It is making clear how different they were though.

Here's the real problem. "Isaac loved Esau; because he had a taste for game" (Gen 25:28). Think of all that is packed into that short phrase. It doesn't say Isaac slightly preferred Esau, but that he loved him. It gives no comment on how he felt about Jacob, which is a powerful comment from silence.

The Bible tells us all we need to know for spiritual life and salvation. It covers thousands of years of human history at minimum. Nonetheless, it is a relatively short book. It is amazing how concise it is. It tends to pack a lot of truth into short sentences at times and this is one of those times.

We must pause and meditate on this phrase and think for a minute what the implications were for young Jacob growing up in this family. His father clearly loved Esau in a way that he did not love Jacob. They were twins. You can't get more like someone else than to be twins. And yet why did dad seem to favor Esau so much more? Was it just because he hunted and cooked tasty food? Was he that shallow? Wasn't he also a great spiritual leader who persevered in prayer for twenty years?

What must have been the thoughts that went through Jacob's tortured little mind? "Why doesn't dad like me? Why do I always get left out? Why do I find it so hard to relate to dad? Why do I freeze up around him? Why do I feel so unsure of myself around him and Esau seems so calm and confident? It's not fair! What's wrong with me?! Why does dad laugh so easily with Esau but rarely with me? Why do we both seem and feel so awkward when we are alone together?" There is a little conjecture here. But he must have felt like the black sheep of the family. He must have felt unloved. He was unloved on some level by his dad.

I hope you can see from all we've studied in this book how easy it would be for Satan to slip into Jacob's young mind and whisper, "If dad doesn't love you, then why should you think God loves you?" Satan isn't mentioned in Jacob's story. But Satan is mentioned in Gen 3, which serves to some degree as the introduction to the whole book of Genesis. It makes all the sense in the world that Satan would be attacking the future head of the Old Testament church, just like he attacked Adam, Job, David (1 Chr 21:1), Jesus, and Peter—other leaders of God's church.

For young children, especially, parents are a real representation of God. The only way they can begin to wrap their little minds around the concept of an all-wise, all-powerful Creator is to think of just a bigger and better dad. Dad is the embodiment of what God is supposed to be for children in their experience. J. Budziszewski, a professor of philosophy at the University of Texas, rightly says, "God is the Father from whom earthly fathers take their name. That is why everything good in a child's earthly father makes it easier for him to love the Father, and why everything bad in him makes it harder."[1] It was meant to be this way. But because of sin, it does not always work well.

I mentioned a woman previously in another chapter who I called Lynn. She grew up in a broken home with a bipolar, abusive mom and a passive, deadbeat dad. Early on a lie came into her mind, which said, "If anything good is to happen in life for me, it's all up to me. If I don't come through and make something happen, it'll never happen." You can see how this is a doubt in the goodness of God, in the goodness of the life God has for you.

To some degree, this lie, like most of Satan's lies, had a lot of truth in it. Often in her family if she didn't work hard and perform well, nothing good would happen for her. It is easy to see how these thoughts about family can get transferred over onto God. This is terrible functional theology. But once it gets baked into your psychological and physiological DNA, it's hard to shake.

Keller has great insight into Jacob and Esau's upbringing:

> Their parents' inordinate, selective love probably accentuated and distorted the temperaments of their sons. . . . Jacob . . . became a calculating, mistrustful, manipulative, insincere man. . . . We must neither feel like complete victims nor like complete villains. . . . We must learn to understand our weaknesses in terms of family patterns. . . . From his earliest days, Jacob seems to have lacked a sense of affirmation and value, and everything in his life is oriented to procuring it. . . . Modern people underestimate the power of affirmative words and condemning words especially from parent to child. Words of blessing and cursing enter into the hearer and have a life and power of their own (cf. James 3:10). . . . Even off-handed comments of criticism and affirmation pass into a child and lodge for years.[2]

---

1. Budziszewski, *Meaning of Sex*, 145.
2. Keller, *What Were We Put in the World to Do?*, 169–76.

What words from your parents have lodged in your soul? Have their offhanded criticisms stayed with you? Did those who raised you seem to bless you or curse you? Have you underestimated the power of condemning words that have been spoken over you? What was the "message" they spoke over your life, even if it was unspoken? What did their attitudes, sighs, facial expressions, body language, and tone of voice "say" to you about you, God, and life in general? What is the main thing in life you are seeking? Why is that?

Many parents read such a quote and instantly think, "I've already ruined my child." Most parents have spoken unnecessary words to their children at some point. If that is you, then confess to God and your child, and work by grace to improve and never do so again. Remember, we are all villains and victims. This is true of you, your parents, and any kids you may have. Your job is to be faithful to live considering the truth you now have. Do not beat yourself up for past sins or wallow in self-pity. Trust the gospel to work miracles in your life and in that of your children.

PRIDE TO PROVIDE FOR SELF

We all struggle with some degree of fear and doubt. It naturally leads to pride if not killed at the deepest root. We think and plan: "If God won't provide for me, I'll provide for myself my own ways! If God doesn't promote me to the positions in life I want, I'll find a way to promote myself. If God won't protect me from harm, then I'll have to do it myself!"

Near the end of Gen 25, we see Jacob and Esau living more as adults but still under their parents' care to some degree. Esau comes home from a failed hunt and is starving. Jacob is making some stew. Esau asks to eat some. Jacob tells Esau he can have some soup in exchange for his birthright. Traditionally, the oldest son got an inheritance twice as big as the other sons. This also set them up to lead the extended family after the father's death.

Esau basically says, "Sure, whatever, who cares; just give me the stew." Jacob seems cold, calculating, and deliberate. It is as if he has been waiting and planning for such an opportunity. He is direct, assertive, and aggressive. He wants a sworn oath. Gordon Wenham says, "The way Jacob states his demand suggests long premeditation and a ruthless exploitation of his brother's moment of weakness."[3] Esau makes the deal.

3. Wenham, *Genesis 16–50*, 178.

Obviously, Jacob did not love his brother. Nor was he trusting God to take care of him and provide for his future inheritance needs. He took matters into his own hands.

Think of David who was anointed to be king by the prophet Samuel while he was a teenager. Yet he had to wait many perilous years to finally ascend the throne. Much of that time, he was on the run from a demon possessed Saul, who tried to kill him. So much of David's godliness was in his faith. He trusted God to provide one day. Therefore, he stayed humble. He didn't rise in pride and demand to have his rights now. He was patient, humble, and content waiting for God's ways and timing. So, too, should we be.

Walter Brueggemann is helpful: "We must believe the promises seriously enough to withstand alternative forms of [provision] which are immediately available and within control. . . . Waiting can be done if one doesn't doubt the outcome."[4] Do you believe strongly in the outcome God has planned for you? This is the key to trusting him, staying humble and patient, and waiting, rather than taking matters into your own hands.

COVETING THE BIRTHRIGHT AND THE BLESSING

In Jacob's day it was the custom for the father to call his family together when he was about to die. He would bless each family member. It was essentially a verbal last will and testament. They rarely used legal contracts on that day. There would have been a meal as the father made official, verbal, legal oaths to his children.

In Gen 27, Isaac is 137 years old. This is how old his older brother, Ishmael, was when he died. Isaac thinks death is near. He is already blind and bedridden. He plans to deliver his last will and testament, but he does not call for the entire family. He only invites Esau. Why is this?

Isaac, late in life, perseveres in his special love for his oldest son. He plans to defy God and his wife and give the blessing to Esau regardless of what God's plan is. He will do it in secret if he must. He invites Esau to cook him a meal and bring it to him alone.

Esau had sold his birthright to Jacob. But the birthright and the father's blessing were essentially the same thing in this case. They were tied together. And if daddy didn't seal the deal, it didn't matter what the two boys had agreed to on their own.

---

4. Brueggemann, *Genesis*, 219–20.

Both sons might get some blessing, but the oldest typically got the biggest and best blessing by far. Isaac plans to give this fuller blessing to Esau. Rebekah, Isaac's wife, wants it for Jacob. God had said Jacob would get the birthright. Jacob longs for it himself.

To bless means to bestow honor, to praise, to endow with a gift, to prosper. It signifies at times a transfer of strength. Blessings in the Old Testament were a much more powerful concept than we often think of. To bless means to do good to someone in a very powerful and generous way.

It was good and right that Jacob wanted the blessing of his father. In fact, God had said he would have it. It is good to desire what God promises us. But Jacob crossed the line from patient waiting and trusting into a demanding, impatient spirit. So much of mature faith is being willing to wait on God's timing and ways. We can often sinfully assume that the good ends justify the sinful means. But they never do. One ounce of sin is never worth it. There are always painful consequences for us and usually for others as well. The pain of the punishment of sin always outlasts the pleasure of sin.

Rebekah, Jacob's mom, overhears Isaac's plan for a lone meeting with Esau. She has a plan to help Jacob get his way. But it is not going to end well.

Jacob had already gotten the birthright from Esau. But it did him no good if his father didn't ratify the deal, so to speak. When we pursue a good thing in a sinful way, we will often get it. But then we won't be able to properly enjoy it. We often get the good thing we covet and then find it's not what we really wanted or needed at the deepest level. Yet in the moment of coveting, we are so blinded by intense desire we press on.

COVERING HIS SHAME AND GUILT TO SELF-PROTECT

Jacob is shrewd. He wants his father's blessing but not his curse. If he is found out in his ruse, a curse may ensue. He tells his concerns to his mom. She comforts him by saying that if dad finds out and curses you, "your curse be on me" (Gen 27:13). This gives him the boldness he needs to move forward.

"The Biblical blessing . . . is a very complex composite of legal action and deep psychological shaping and prophetic insight into the future."[5] These were not mere words. There was power in this blessing. There

---

5. Keller, *What Were We Put in the World to Do?*, 177.

was profit as well because he would inherit much of his dad's property. All these are good things in and of themselves, but they can't satisfy the depths of the human soul. Still, Jacob pressed ahead.

Rebekah's plan is to cook a goat in such a way that Isaac will think it is game that Esau has cooked for him. Jacob is worried that his mother's plan won't work. He thinks his father will discover the ruse because Esau is hairy and Jacob has smooth skin.

Mom has a plan for that as well. She covers Jacob's skin with animal hide so that he feels hairy all over. Quite literally they develop a plan to cover their sin. She cooks a tasty meal for her husband. She dresses Jacob in Esau's finest festival robe.

We may stop at this point and think to ourselves, "I don't go through all these elaborate schemes to cover my sin." Oh, no? Watch what Jacob does next. As he walks into his father's tent he lies over and over telling his blind father that he is Esau. Maybe the greatest way we still seek to cover our sin today is with our lies—subtle, small, white though they may be. We hide behind the lies of our own righteousness. We think to ourselves, "As long as my spouse, my kids, my boss, friends, and neighbors don't know, I can hold on to my sense of dignity and uprightness." We think we must constantly put our best foot, which is our false foot, forward. We lie, we hide, we minimize, we cover up, and we rationalize. We think we must do this to gain a blessing in life.

APPLICATION

In some sense Jacob's plan works. He gets the blessing from his father. But in another sense, it did not work. Esau quickly learns of it and is so mad he plans to kill Jacob. To protect him, Rebekah sends him away to live with relatives for a while. She probably thinks it will be a very short visit.

What good is a blessing and family inheritance if you aren't around to inherit it? He wouldn't be there to obtain all the land and property he had just won through his lies. When we live a life of doubt, pride, coveting, and covering, we will often get exactly what we want. And then we will find it was not worth all the trouble. This ought to be a sobering warning for us all. When you pursue something, even the right something, in a sinful way, you will push yourself further from experiencing the very good thing you want.

Instead of living by a fear that God won't bless us, we must live by faith that he deeply wants to bless us and will. Instead of living by hubris and pride that seeks to provide for ourselves, we must stay humble and trust God to provide in his best way and time and place. Instead of coveting and lusting after God's good gifts, we must learn to stay content with the ones we presently have, trusting his plan and timing. The life of faith is a waiting game. We often get into sin by getting into a hurry and demanding a right thing, right now, instead of being content to wait for God's timetable to play out.

CONCLUSION

This is a sad story, and, in some ways, it gets worse before it gets better. Jacob will be gone for twenty years. When he returns, his mother is dead. He will never see again in this life the parent who was so close to him. Sin never works out in the long run.

This is a sober story to end up with because there really is no good guy in the whole story. Jacob, Esau, Isaac, and Rebekah all come off as short-sighted, fearful, selfish, demanding sinners. But there is something truly beautiful here, even amidst all the pain.

All our sin starts with doubt that God will provide for us what we most need in life. Now that we are all ruined in sin and shame, what we most need is to be covered. Yet as saw back in Gen 3 our attempts to cover ourselves never work. We can't provide true covering for ourselves. But Christ can.

Esau wasn't a great older brother. He showed no love for Jacob in all this. Isaac wasn't a great father. But Isaac loved Esau greatly and thus Esau had free access to his father.

Jacob lived his whole life wanting his father's blessing and smile. He worked so hard to obtain it. But he couldn't get it on his own.

Christ is the true older brother, perfect in love for all his younger siblings. He was neither selfish nor fearful. He did not grasp onto his rights, privileges, birthrights, and blessings. He was so full of life and love he longed to share his blessings with all his people.

Christ came to the earth. He said that if there must be a curse on his people, it could fall on him. It did. Because of his great sacrificial love and death, we can now cover ourselves in his royal righteous robe by faith. We literally can put on his righteous life like clothes to wear into our Father's house.

Now by faith we can approach our all-seeing, all-knowing Father, and he delights in us! Jacob deeply and desperately wanted his father's smile and blessing. He never fully, really got it. But in Christ, we can approach our Father and have his full smile and deep blessing eternally!

The Father's justice is assuaged by his Son's sacrifice in our place. Now his love flows freely to us. He delights in us fully. He embraces us. He smells the freshness of Christ on us. He blesses us for all eternity.

Let the reality of the gospel shine brightly in your life. When temptations to doubt, fear, pride, and coveting come, turn by faith to Christ. Look long and hard at your glorious Savior. Rest in him. Let fear turn to faith, pride to peace, and coveting to contentment. Hallelujah! What a Savior.

Conclusion

Matthew 9:2-8

Four men brought a paralytic friend, lying on a mat, to see Jesus one day. Every indication is that they, and most likely their friend, were coming to Jesus wanting a miraculous healing. But at first Jesus did not give that. At first, he merely pronounced the man's sins forgiven. Later, to make a point to the Pharisees, he did heal the man.

One thing this passage seems to teach is that the greatest need of all humans is to be forgiven by God. Even if you are crippled from the neck down, forgiveness is the most important thing. Even if you are crippled by remaining sin in your life, being forgiven of sin by God, is more important than being healed in the here and now from all your sinful tendencies.

Don't get me wrong. Being practically healed from sin's indwelling power is supremely important. God promises to do that for all believers. It will be fully and perfectly done in the next life. It will be partially and progressively done in this life as Rom 8:3-4 shows. This book aims to help you attack sin at its deepest root level and kill as much of it there in your heart's beliefs before sin ever grows to full bloom in your feelings, desires, words, and actions. Hopefully the truths in this book will speed you along the path of progressively killing your sin. But the work will never be done in this life. If we live to be one hundred and twenty years old, we will still struggle with some sin then.

So, as you seek to apply the truths in this book, don't grow weary or discouraged. Don't give up. Don't lose heart. Even on the days you fail to beat sin and fall again into the same old pattern of believing lies, remember the greatest truth of all: Christ died for sinners. If you trust in him to save you, he will forgive all your sins, past, present, and future, even as you continue to struggle. Press on in his grace.

Appendix A

Sinful Self-Protective Strategies

Genesis 3:7–14

What follows is a list of different ways people will try to avoid having to admit and repent of their sin. There is some overlap between some of these. The list is certainly not exhaustive. John MacArthur teaches that all humanity is reluctant to admit our sin.[1] Here are different crafty ways we hide our sin or at least avoid having to talk about it out loud to other humans.

PUT OUR BEST FOOT FORWARD

1. Messiah complex:

    a. "I always wanted to be a life giver, never a life taker." They love to minister to others struggling with sin but refuse to admit their weakness so anyone can minister to them.

2. I'm never wrong:

    a. "If you're not for me you're against me. I'm the leader; get in line and obey."

    b. Lying or "misremembering" what happened. "I don't remember ever saying that!"

    c. "Others just don't understand, if they did, they'd see it my way." Essentially, "I'm smarter than you."

---

1. MacArthur, *Study Bible*, 20.

3. Focus on the positive/good outweighs the bad:
    a. "Bring a good report; let's not focus on the bad!"
    b. "I've already made progress in that area, so we don't need to discuss that again. I'm past that, right?"
    c. "I'm on a mission; God's doing so much. I can't slow down to deal with this. Don't hinder God's work!"
4. Always the teacher:
    a. They love to talk deeply about other people's sins, just never their own.

PUT OUR FEAR FORWARD

5. I'm trying: "I already know; you don't have to tell me again. I'm getting better, or I will get better."
6. I'm hurt: "Maybe there is some sin there, but that's not the main point. My pain is the main thing!"
7. Ostrich: They pretend it's not there. They try to ignore or overlook all the obvious evidence. Denial.
8. No vulnerability: They will often talk openly about their sin, but they refuse to listen and change.

PUT OUR EXCUSES FORWARD

9. Secondary issues / that's not my gifting: They talk about personality traits and preferences, but never sin.
10. Minimizer (there are multiple ways to do this one):
    a. Some people joke and make light of it. They don't take anything too serious. They treat their sin as small.
    b. Some just say, "I know it's there, but it isn't that bad, it's gotten a lot better. Let's drop it for now, OK?"
11. Vague generalizer: They will say, "We're all sinners," but refuse to say, "I sinned in that instance."

12. Blame shifter: They will do anything to get the spotlight off themselves:

    a. Counter puncher: Someone accuses them of sin; they are quick to accuse that person back.

    b. Not my fault / misdirection: "Yes, I did that, but you must understand the circumstances that led to it."

    c. My intentions were good: "They misunderstood my intentions."

Appendix B

Confronting Someone in Order to Forgive Them and Set Boundaries

Please pray before, during, and after this process for the best results! Pray for wisdom and blessing.

1. Thank them for all the good you honestly can. For example: "Thanks for always providing for me, etc . . ."
2. Ask them to listen first. Promise them they will have time to respond. "Please let me get this all out."
3. Briefly describe the current situation and relationship. "Things have been tense with us, etc . . ."
4. Say something positive about them that is hopeful. "I think you really still want a good relationship with me."
5. Tell them the things they are doing to you that are sinful. Give themes and examples. Try to get all the current sins and themes out there. It's ideal if you can back them all up with a verse.
    a. "You often assume the worst about me" (1 Cor 13:7). For example: "Mom said something negative about me and you believed her without asking me first."
    b. "You often blame shift the tension in our relationship as though it's all my fault" (Gen 3:11–14). For example: "You say I never come to see you, but you never come to see me either. We're both guilty."

CONFRONTING SOMEONE IN ORDER TO FORGIVE THEM AND SET BOUNDARIES

6. Tell them the kind of relationship you want with them. Ideally this is one of love, trust, and respect.
7. Detail the sinful things they have done in the past if they have not been genuinely repented of. (Follow the example in point 5.)
8. Detail the new boundaries you are setting. It is probably best to have decided these beforehand and not come in willing to negotiate the boundaries at this point.
   a. If you start to use harsh language with me, I will walk out of the room or hang up the phone.
   b. If you start to blame shift your sin to me, I will walk out of the room or hang up the phone.
   c. If you say something negative to my kids about me, we will hang up or leave your house immediately.
9. Give them a chance to respond.
10. Pray for a new and better relationship in closing.

In closing, it would be ideal to write down all you want to say for three reasons at least:

1. Do this so that you can be clear and confident ahead of time.
2. If you get flustered, your notes should help you be able to stay focused.
3. If they get belligerent or overly emotional and you must walk away, you can just hand them the letter.

Appendix C

Satan's Five Main Lies and Accusations and Our Responses

SATAN SAYS:

1. God's not good enough:
    a. His word is not trustworthy.
    b. His power and consequences aren't trustworthy.
    c. His love is not trustworthy.
2. You're not good enough.
3. Life's not good enough.
4. The gospel is not good enough to cover your sins.
5. The gospel is not good enough to cover others' sins against you so that you can forgive them.

OUR RIGHT RESPONSE:

1. Faith: God is wise, strong, and loving. I trust him.
2. Humility: I have all that's best for me in Christ right now. I can wait on his timing and ways.
3. Contentment: Only God will satisfy. I will look to him ultimately for joy.

4. Christ: Only he can cover my sin, guilt, and shame.
5. Grace: I should, can, and will forgive as I've been forgiven.

OUR SINFUL RESPONSE

1. Fear: God won't provide for, protect, and or promote me as he should.
2. Hubris: Therefore, I must provide for, protect, and or promote myself.
3. Covet: Things in this life will fully satisfy me.
4. Cover: I must cover my sin, guilt, and shame somehow on my own.
5. Grudges: I must never fully forgive others, or they may hurt me again.

Appendix D

Overview and Summary

1. We are sinned against by Satan. Sin starts with Satan (Gen 3:1–14).

    a. First lie: God's not good. He doesn't protect, provide, and promote as he should.

    b. Second lie: You're not good. You lack something you ought to have or need to have.

    c. Third lie: Life's not good. You're getting a raw deal from God. Life should be better.

    d. Fourth lie: The gospel is not good enough for you. You must cover and save yourself.

    e. Fifth lie: The gospel is not good enough for others. Don't forgive those who've hurt you.

2. Our sinful responses:

    a. Doubt and fear: God won't protect, provide for, or promote me in the best ways (Rom 14:23).

    b. Pride/hubris: If God won't protect, provide for, and promote me, then I must do so for myself.

    c. Coveting: I have good God-given desires for security, satisfaction, and significance. I must get possessions, passion, pleasure, power/prestige or fortune, fulfillment, fame/followers by any means necessary, even if I must sin to do it (Gen 3:6; Matt 4:3–8; 1 John 2:16).

d. Covering: I must cover up my own sin and shame (Gen 3:7–13).

   e. Holding a grudge: I must protect myself from others by not forgiving them (Heb 12:15).

3. Guilt and shame resulting from our sin lead us to attempt to cover our sin, guilt, and shame.

   a. We hide from others by putting our best foot forward, or doing righteous deeds (Gen 3:7).

   b. We hide from God by putting fear forward (Gen 3:8–10).

   c. We hide from ourselves by putting excuses forward, minimizing, or blame shifting (Gen 3:11–12).

4. Sinful self-protection from the pain, pressure, guilt, and shame of life may seem to work for a while. But it never lasts (Gen 3:7–14).

   a. We give into the lie: I am apathetic, under functioning, and live like a libertine and a victim.

   b. We fight the lie in sinful strength: I am anxious, over functioning, am legalistic, and a self-made person.

5. The right way to fight against these lies and sinful strategies is with the word, prayer, fellowship, worship (2 Cor 10:3–5).

Appendix E

Questions to Ask Yourself and Others to Help Discern Personalized Lies

1. What's the main lie and or accusation you hear from Satan in your mind most often, the negative self-talk, reoccurring mantra?
2. When was the first time or the main time you remember hearing it in life? It doesn't have to be dramatic to be traumatic.
3. Do you have any bitterness, grudges, ongoing anger towards anyone you've ever heard the lie or accusation through, such as a parent, sibling, relative, coach, teacher, boss, or friend?
4. When do you hear or feel this lie most often in present day life and circumstances?
5. If you're in the flesh, how do you typically respond to the lie? Do you give into it or fight it? How specifically?
6. If you're in the Spirit, how do you tend to respond to the lie?
7. What biblical truths best help you fight the lie? Ask God to give you a personalized verse to fight.

Bibliography

Augustine. *The City of God*. Translated by Marcus Dods. New York: Random House, 1993.
Boice, James Montgomery. *Genesis*. Vol. 1. Grand Rapids: Baker, 2002.
Brock, Michael. *8 Errors Parents Make*. Moscow, ID: Canon, 2024.
Brooks, Thomas. *Precious Remedies Against Satan's Devices*. Carlisle, PA: Banner of Truth Trust, 2000.
Bruce, F. F. *The Epistles to the Colossians, to Philemon, and to the Ephesians*. Grand Rapids: Eerdmans, 1984.
Brueggemann, Walter. *Genesis*. Louisville: Westminster John Knox, 2010.
Budziszewski, J. *On the Meaning of Sex*. Wilmington, DE: Intercollegiate Studies Institute, 2017.
Burroughs, Jeremiah. *The Rare Jewel of Christian Contentment*. Edinburgh: Banner of Truth Trust, 1979.
Calvin, John. *Commentaries on the Twelve Minor Prophets*. Vol. 5. Grand Rapids: Baker, 2003.
———. *Ephesians*. Grand Rapids: Baker, 2003.
———. *Genesis*. Vol. 1. Grand Rapids: Baker, 2003.
———. *Harmony of the Evangelists*. Vol. 1. Grand Rapids: Baker, 2003.
———. *Harmony of the Evangelists*. Vol. 3. Grand Rapids: Baker, 2003.
———. *Sermons on 2 Samuel*. Translated by Douglas Kelly. Carlise, PA: Banner of Truth Trust, 1992.
Carson, D. A. *Matthew: Chapters 1 Through 12*. Grand Rapids: Zondervan, 1995.
———. *Matthew: Chapters 13 Through 28*. Grand Rapids: Zondervan, 1995.
Comer, John Mark. *Live No Lies*. New York: WaterBrook, 2021.
DeYoung, Kevin. *The Good News We Almost Forgot*. Chicago: Moody, 2010.
Evagrius of Pontus. *Talking Back: A Monastic Handbook for Combating Demons*. Translated by David Brakke. Collegeville, MN: Liturgical, 2009.
Ferguson, Sinclair B. *The Christian Life*. Carlise, PA: Banner of Truth Trust, 2023.
———. *The Whole Christ*. Wheaton, IL: Crossway, 2016.
Fisher, Edward. *The Marrow of Modern Divinity*. Tain, UK: Christian Heritage, 2009.

BIBLIOGRAPHY

France, R. T. *Matthew*. Grand Rapids: Eerdmans, 2007.
Gil, John. *Exposition of the New Testament*. Vol. 3. Paris, AK: Baptist Standard Bearer, 2006.
Hamilton, Victor P. *The Book of Genesis: Chapters 1–17*. Grand Rapids: Eerdmans, 1990.
Hendriksen, William. *Matthew*. Grand Rapids: Baker, 2002.
Henry, Matthew. *The NIV Matthew Henry Commentary*. Grand Rapids: Zondervan, 1992.
Howard, Joshua P. *The Exorcism of Satan*. Conway, AR: Free Grace, 2022.
Keil, C. F., and F. Delitzsch. *Commentary on the Old Testament*. Vol. 10. Translated by James Martin. Grand Rapids: Eerdmans.
Keller, Timothy. *Counterfeit Gods*. New York: Penguin, 2009.
———. *Forgive: Why Should I and How Can I?* New York: Viking, 2022.
———. *The Prodigal Prophet*. New York: Viking, 2018.
———. *What Were We Put in the World to Do? Leader's Guide*. New York: Redeemer Presbyterian Church, 2006.
Key, Harrison Scott. *How to Stay Married*. New York: Avid Reader, 2023.
Kidner, Derek. *Genesis*. Downers Grove, IL: IVP Academic, 1967.
———. *The Wisdom of Proverbs, Job, and Ecclesiastes*. Downers Grove, IL: InterVarsity, 1985.
Kistemaker, Simon J. *Exposition of James, Epistles of John, Peter, and Jude*. Grand Rapids: Baker, 2002.
Knox, John. *Writings of the Rev. John Knox*. London: Religious Tract Society, 1830.
Lemmel, Helen H. "Turn Your Eyes upon Jesus." In *The Hymnal for Worship and Celebration*, 335. Waco, TX: Word, 1986.
Lewis, C. S. *The Christian Life*. Carlisle, PA: Banner of Truth Trust, 2023.
———. *The Inspirational Writings*. New York: Inspirational, 1994.
———. *The Problem of Pain*. London, UK: Geoffrey Bles, 1940.
———. *The Screwtape Letters*. New York: Macmillan, 1982.
Lloyd-Jones, D. Martyn. *The Christian Warfare*. Grand Rapids: Baker, 2003.
———. *Spiritual Depressions*. Grand Rapids: Zondervan, 2002.
Lovelace, Richard. *Dynamics of Spiritual Life*. Downers Grove, IL: InterVaristy, 1979.
Luther, Martin. *Galatians*. Grand Rapids: Revell, 1999.
MacArthur, John. *Ephesians*. Chicago: Moody, 1986.
———. *James*. Chicago: Moody, 1998.
———. *Luke 11–17*. Chicago: Moody, 2013.
———. *The MacArthur Study Bible*. Nashville: Word, 1997.
Manchester, William. *The Last Lion*. Vol. 1. Boston: Little, Brown, 1983.
Manton, Thomas. *James*. Lafayette, IN: Sovereign Grace, 2001.
Owen, John. *Sin and Temptation: The Challenge of Personal Godliness*. Edited by James M. Houston. Minneapolis: Bethany House, 1996.
Peterson, Andrée Seu. "Poisonous Thoughts: Escaping the Kingdom of 'Noise,' Part 1." *World Magazine*, May 18, 2024, 70.
Piper, John. *Living in the Light: Money, Sex, and Power*. Charlotte, NC: Good Book, 2016.
———. *Providence*. Wheaton, IL: Crossway, 2020.
———. "The Word of God: Living, Active, Sharp." Desiring God. Sermon, 41:26. Recorded Sept. 8, 1996. https://www.desiringgod.org/messages/the-word-of-god-living-active-sharp.

Poole, Matthew. *A Commentary on the Holy Bible*. Vol. 1. Peabody, MA: Hendrickson, 1985.

———. *A Commentary on the Holy Bible*. Vol. 3. Peabody, MA: Hendrickson, 1985.

Robinson, Robert. "Come, Thou Fount of Every Blessing." In *The Hymnal for Worship and Celebration*, 2. Waco, TX: Word, 1986.

Shirmer, Ted. *The Freedom Fight*. Houston, TX: High Bridge, 2020.

Stott, John. *The Message of Ephesians*. Downers Grove, IL: InterVarsity, 1979.

———. *The Message of Romans*. Downers Grove, IL: InterVarsity, 1994.

Stubbs, Olan. *Forgiveness*. Self-published, Amazon Digital Services, 2022.

———. *Truth Wars*. Self-published, Amazon Digital Services, 2022.

Tripp, Paul David. *Lead: 12 Gospel Principles for Leadership in the Church*. Wheaton, IL: Crossway, 2020.

Watson, Thomas. *The Lord's Prayer*. London: Banner of Truth Trust, 1956.

Wenham, G. J. "Genesis." In *New Bible Commentary*, edited by D. A. Carson et al., 54–91. Downers Grove, IL: InterVarsity, 2004.

———. *Genesis 1–15*. Vol. 1. Word Biblical Commentary. Grand Rapids: Zondervan, 1987.

———. *Genesis 16–50*. Grand Rapids: Zondervan, 2000.

Westermann, Claus. *Genesis 1–11*. A Continental Commentary. Minneapolis: Fortress, 1994.

Wiersbe, Warren. *Be Rich*. Colorado Springs: David C. Cook, 2009.

Willard, Dallas. *Renovation of the Heart: Putting on the Character of Christ*. Colorado Springs: NavPress, 2002.

www.ingramcontent.com/pod-product-compliance
Lightning Source LLC
Chambersburg PA
CBHW062042220426
43662CB00010B/1615